D0652639

Chinese Astrology

Exploring the Eastern Zodiac

By Shelly Wu

New Page Books
A division of The Career Press, Inc.
Franklin Lakes, NJ

SOMERSET CO. LIBRARY
BRIDGEWATER, N.J. 08807

Copyright © 2005 by Shelly Wu

All rights reserved under the Pan-American and International Copyright Conventions. This book may not be reproduced, in whole or in part, in any form or by any means electronic or mechanical, including photocopying, recording, or by any information storage and retrieval system now known or hereafter invented, without written permission from the publisher, The Career Press.

CHINESE ASTROLOGY
EDITED AND TYPESET BY CHRISTOPHER CAROLEI
ORIGINAL ARTWORK BY SHERIDAH D. DAVIS AND ROBERT R. LANGWELL
Cover design by Lu Rossman/Digi Dog Design
Printed in the U.S.A. by Book-mart Press

To order this title, please call toll-free 1-800-CAREER-1 (NJ and Canada: 201-848-0310) to order using VISA or MasterCard, or for further information on books from Career Press.

The Career Press, Inc., 3 Tice Road, PO Box 687,
Franklin Lakes, NJ 07417
www.careerpress.com
www.newpagebooks.com

Library of Congress Cataloging-in-Publication Data

Wu, Shelly, 1959-
    Chinese astrology : exploring the eastern zodiac / by Shelly Wu.
        p. cm.
    Includes index.
    ISBN 1-56414-796-7
    1. Astrology, Chinese. I. Title.

BF1714.C5W795 2005
133.5'9251--dc21

2004058460

Dedication

Losing my mother was a defining moment in my life. When this happened, I found myself faced with the daunting task of going through and distributing her personal belongings. Each closet I opened became more difficult as I pictured her wearing each flowered dress.

Despite being a grown woman, on that day I was no more than a grieving child. I buried my face into the clothing, which still smelled of her perfume—the loss was almost unbearable. I knew that her mother, my maternal grandmother, was a poet and a Goat born in 1907. In a weathered nightstand amongst my mother's belongings, I found both her's and my grandmother's poetry. My tears were replaced by a smile as I read the tattered piece of paper that was addressed to me:

They say you are a tom boy child,
Small daughter of the wind;
With clothes awry, and hair blown wild,
Your hands and knees well-skinned.

You do not play with dolls, or sit
And meekly learn to sew;
Because you do not care one bit
What little girls should know.

You gather creatures you have found
Along your gypsy roads;
A fallen bird...a sorry hound...
Or "needy" cats and toads.

You love to face a bully's threat
And stand up to his dare;
Or see that others don't forget
The rules of "playing fair."

But sometimes in your wanderings,
You cause us real alarm;
You seem to think God gave you wings
Instead of girlish charm!

Until you grow into your teens,
When boys begin to care.
It's then you'll give up bugs and jeans,
For flowers in your hair!

My grandmother wrote this poem for me when I was a young girl, but I had never seen it. I was dumbstruck to read this perfect description of a child born into a Dog year. These are amazing insights, considering she had no knowledge of astrology. Perhaps all truth is indeed universal and stands the test of time.

I would like to dedicate this book to my mother, whose insightful poetry is used throughout the book; to my grandmother, who taught me to love words; and to my father, who introduced me to the spiritual world. Finally, I wish to dedicate this book to my precious children: Sheridah, Tyler, and Katie Rose. My writing is a part of me, but *you* are the best of me.

Acknowledgments

My deepest thanks to the irrepressible Linda Marie Stein, Ph.D., for her assistance with the book, her encouragement, and her friendship.

Thank you to our Goat-year artist, Sheridah Davis, for the beautiful artwork throughout the book.

And a special thanks to my long-suffering Aristotle. Why can't all men be Pigs?

Contents

Preface   9

Introduction   11

Chapter 1   What Is Chinese Astrology?   13

Chapter 2   The 12 Signs of the Eastern Zodiac   17

Chapter 3   The Rat   23

Chapter 4   The Ox   35

Chapter 5   The Tiger   47

Chapter 6   The Rabbit/Cat   57

Chapter 7   The Dragon   69

Chapter 8   The Snake   81

Chapter 9   The Horse   93

Chapter 10   The Goat/Sheep   105

Chapter 11   The Monkey   117

Chapter 12   The Rooster   129

Chapter 13   The Dog   141

Chapter 14   The Pig/Boar   153

Chapter 15   The Elements   163

Chapter 16   Your Birth Time Companion   189

Chapter 17   Chinese Love Signs—
                      Karmic Connections   195

Chapter 18   Quick Reference Guide to the 12 Signs
                      of the Eastern Zodiac   235

Endnotes   249

Index   251

About the Author   255

Preface

Within this book is the knowledge that each of us is a combination of light and darkness, and that we are capable of functioning either at a higher vibrational level of love and acceptance, or choosing to use our lower-level base personality, which can be unenlightened and petty.

No astrological sign is superior to another. Together they swirl like a kaleidoscope of beautiful colors, standing in contrast to gray shadows. We will learn that we control our own destinies to a great degree.

If I have done my job, after reading this book you will have learned that bombastic boss of yours may very well be a Tiger or a Dragon; your demure librarian a Rabbit or a Snake; your fun-loving friend a Monkey, and your methodical, hardworking business associate an Ox.

I hope that you will have a better understanding of your own temperament, and those of your friends and loved ones. It is only with understanding that we come to accept ourselves and those around us. The purpose of this book is to give you some "aha!" moments about yourself and those whom you meet along life's path.

Introduction

He who knows others is learned, he who knows himself is wise.
—Lao-tse

The quest for self-knowledge and personal identity has been a universal human pursuit for millenniums. Who are we, and could our destiny be written in the stars? Why do some commit their wings to life's flames, while others tiptoe through life so cautiously?

In the quest for answers to these questions, there has been an explosion of renewed interest in Chinese astrology. Awareness of our essential nature aids in self-acceptance and enlightenment, and provides insight into our most intimate relationships.

Many of us are familiar with Western astrology. We can read our sun signs in the daily newspapers and even buy magazines and periodicals that offer predictions based on our sun and rising signs. However, there is another form of astrology known as Chinese or Eastern astrology. Chinese astrology is based on 12 archetypal temperaments represented by each of 12 symbolic animal signs.

Eastern astrology differs from popular Western astrology in many ways. While this lunar-based system utilizes fixed mathematical formulas, it is not entirely a science of forecasting, but rather an interpretive art. Chinese astrology is built upon foundations of principle, order, and the spiritual laws of synchronicity (or the theory of "meaningful coincidences"). This is the journey of the spirit through the physical dimension. It is said that we plot the characteristics of our personality and determine the purpose for our present existence. Truly, our character reflects the intent of our spirit.

11

Utilizing 5,000 years of practical observations, Chinese astrology reveals the attributes, driving forces, and possibilities that your birth year offers you. Throughout the centuries, multitudes have delved into the mysteries that underlie their personalities. This is a timeless system that is as pertinent today as it was many centuries ago.

The Chinese speak of one's "natural endowment" or "inner being." There are two faces that make up our personality. The first is *xian tian*, or our original inherent "temperament." These are the spiritual attributes that we came into this life with—our personality from the beginning. The second is *hou tian*, or our acquired "character." This is determined by our choices and conduct.

What is "temperament," and what relationship does it have to "character" in forming the personality? Temperament is our inclinations, tendencies, and predisposition. Character is a collection of actual habits and behaviors—our actual disposition. Temperament plus character equals personality. Personality traits (patterns of thinking, perceiving, and reacting), are relatively stable over time.

As you explore each sign, notice if you see similarities between people you know and try to guess their Chinese astrological sign. After learning about these ancient personality archetypes, you may notice some interesting similarities to your friends and family; and quite possibly, you may never look at yourself the same way again.

Chapter 1

What Is Chinese Astrology?

To know a man's character,
See what he does,
Mark his motives,
Examine in what things he rests.
—Confucius

The Eastern Zodiac is perhaps the oldest known horoscope system in the world. Ancient writings have been dated as early as the fourth millennium B.C., many of which have been well-preserved and can be found in the monasteries of Tibet, China, and southeast Asia.

In ancient China, the spiritual teachers of the time were responsible for maintaining the stability and the well-being of the population. After many centuries of recording seasonal, agricultural, astronomical, and physical cycles, theories concerning human nature also began to develop.

The roots of the Chinese astrological system are planted deeply in the classical philosophies of Kongzi (Confucius) and Laozi (Lao Tse). These leaders became the first recorded psychologists and counselors of the time. The art of character reading developed as the Chinese writing system emerged, and eventually merged with the philosophy of the time.

This psychological folk wisdom developed and was passed along orally beginning as early as 500 B.C. It was eventually refined and documented in the text of the Yi Jing (I Ching), or "Book of Changes." The insights into one's character, lifestyle, and emotional makeup are uncanny.

We are each born with a certain ming (destiny) in this life. The Chinese phrase for fate is ming yun. This is said to be an individual's life purpose, or the reason for their present existence. Fate occurs when events happen as intended. Tian ming is our destiny, or our "daily lot in life," when our fate (soul and spirit) is in harmony with our earthly personality.

The term "luck" is a rather unclear expression. Most of us know what luck is and are accutely aware of when it is good or bad. Although this luck cannot be seen, it is profoundly evident in our daily lives. In Eastern philosophy there is said to be three types of luck. "Heaven luck" is our fate, the big picture, the framework or spiritual roadmap of our life. "Man luck" is our destiny, the choices that we make, and the effort we put forth working within our intrinsic framework. "Earth luck" is the manipulation of our luck via the arranging of our environment (thereby altering the energy of external influences using tools such as feng shui[1]).

Physicists tell us that "for every action, there is an equal and opposite reaction." The laws of nature that apply to earthly physics function in a similar fashion throughout the spiritual world. Chinese astrology is a form of "spiritual quantum physics." Just as gravity plummets an object to the ground, so the laws of spiritual physics dictate that for every act there is a logical consequence. In this way, we shape our own destiny through our free will, and by way of the choices we make.

Each sign, or archetype, is a balanced mixture of positive and negative attributes. The Tiger's courage and bravery can also be manifest as haste, or action without forethought. The Dog's watchfulness and loyalty can become hypervigilance and possessiveness. The Rabbit's good manners and refinement can also be expressed as timidity and detachment. Those personality traits that we would naturally view as positive ones (loyalty, forgiveness, compassion) reflect alignment of our personality with our spirit (Qi). Those traits we would view as negative (anger, jealousy, bitterness) reflect a great separation between the human personality and our spiritual essence. The greater the gulf between spirit and personality, the darker one's character.

The ancient Chinese attributed the origin of all life to the balance between heaven and Earth, and the yin and the yang. The yin represents the negative, passive night-force; it is female, watery, and receiving. The yang represents the positive, aggressive day force; it is male, firey, and giving. These two halves are represented in the familiar Chinese symbol known as the Tai Qi, or the Yin and Yang.

Qi (pronounced Chee) is the life force itself. It is the combination of "heaven luck" (divine spirit) and "man, or earth luck" (human personality). One yin and one yang are called "Tao." Meaning "the way," Tao is the ancient Chinese term for the ordering principle that makes harmony possible. In the ancient text of the Tao Te Jing, the Chinese philosopher Lao Tse formulated a philosophical system that introduced the concept of health and prosperity through awareness of the natural cosmic cycles. This awareness of life, he suggested, was the path to finding "balance" and achieving a "satisfied mind." According to this principle, the Tao gives birth to one perfect whole that carries the yin on its back and embraces yang in its arms. This blending of Qi then becomes balanced and harmonious. Yin and yang are the Tao of heaven and of Earth. This is the principle and root beginning of life and death, of mother and father, and of spiritual enlightenment.

Although we mortals live on Earth, our life is suspended from heaven. We are, indeed, spiritual creatures contained within a physical body. When heaven and Earth combine Qi, this is called life. All living things need Qi to survive and to run their life cycles. Qi brings both good and bad fortunes. "Sheng Qi" is positive. It is present when we are happy, healthy, and flourishing in a balanced environment. "Si Qi" is a mixture of good and bad energy. It is present when we are weak or depleted, but basically at a status quo. "Sha Qi" is negative energy and is present when we experience extreme anger, illness, or misfortunes (such as disrupted relationships, professional or financial calamity, malevolent spirits, and death).

Some may find themselves born into an animal year that does not sound particularly flattering. A sign such as the Dragon sounds very majestic and important. Other signs (the Pig, for instance) seem somehow less impressive. Each animal designation is a symbolic archetype and represents a specific behavioral psychology. It could perhaps be called the Myers-Briggs[2] personality inventory of Eastern philosophy. Each personality style fulfills an essential place in the balance of the universe.

The Asian Zodiac uses calculations of yearly or lunar year periods, rather than months to order the signs. Each of the 12 animal signs lasts for an entire year, beginning on various dates between mid-January and mid-February. Each sign repeats every 12th year, but the specific combination of animal sign and element occurs only once every 60 years.

My wish for you, the reader, is to discover this ancient treasure trove of knowledge, and the hidden forces that underlie your personality. Have fun as you begin this adventure, and may you enjoy your journey on this "search for self."

Chapter 2

The 12 Signs of the Eastern Zodiac

The wise person does not lay up treasure; their riches lie within.
—Lao-tse

The Symbolic Parable

According to legend, the order of the 12 signs of Chinese astrology was determined by Buddha. Upon celebration of the Chinese New Year (which falls on different dates, from mid-January to mid-February), all of the animals in the kingdom were invited, but only 12 creatures attended.

The first animal to arrive was the intellectual, talkative Rat, who was aggressive enough to jump off the back of the Ox, and thus the first to arrive.

The next to come was the hardworking Ox, followed by the active Tiger, and the detached Rabbit (or Cat). The outspoken Dragon joined the others, as did the wise and philosophical Snake. The physically active Horse trotted in with his good friend the artistic Goat.

The irrepressible Monkey and the candid Rooster arrived as well. The last to join the others were the watchful Dog and the resigned Pig.

The legend continues that each animal acquired a year of its own, bestowing their symbolic nature and characteristics to those born in that animal's year. It is the untamed force concealed within you—your inner self from the beginning.

Find Your Chinese Birth Sign

From	To	Element	Animal
January 30, 1881	February 17, 1882	Metal	Snake
February 18, 1882	January 7, 1883	Water	Horse
February 8, 1883	January 27, 1884	Water	Goat
January 28, 1884	February 14, 1885	Wood	Monkey
February 15, 1885	February 3, 1886	Wood	Rooster
February 4, 1886	January 23, 1887	Fire	Dog
January 24, 1887	February 11, 1888	Fire	Pig
February 12, 1888	January 30, 1889	Earth	Rat
January 31, 1889	January 20, 1890	Earth	Ox
January 21, 1890	February 19, 1891	Metal	Tiger
February 20, 1891	January 29, 1892	Metal	Rabbit
January 30, 1892	February 16, 1893	Water	Dragon
February 17, 1893	February 5, 1894	Water	Snake
February 6, 1894	January 25, 1895	Wood	Horse
January 26, 1895	February 12, 1896	Wood	Goat
February 13, 1896	February 1, 1897	Fire	Monkey
February 2, 1897	January 21, 1898	Fire	Rooster
January 22, 1898	February 9, 1899	Earth	Dog
February 10, 1899	January 30, 1900	Earth	Pig
January 31, 1900	February 18, 1901	Metal	Rat
February 19, 1901	February 7, 1902	Metal	Ox
February 8, 1902	January 28, 1903	Water	Tiger
January 29, 1903	February 15, 1904	Water	Rabbit
February 16, 1904	February 3, 1905	Wood	Dragon
February 4, 1905	January 24, 1906	Wood	Snake
January 25, 1906	February 12, 1907	Fire	Horse
February 13, 1907	February 1, 1908	Fire	Goat
February 2, 1908	January 21, 1909	Earth	Monkey
January 22, 1909	February 9, 1910	Earth	Rooster
February 10, 1910	January 29, 1911	Metal	Dog
January 30, 1911	February 17, 1912	Metal	Pig
February 18, 1912	February 5, 1913	Water	Rat
February 6, 1913	January 25, 1914	Water	Ox

Find Your Chinese Birth Sign

From	To	Element	Animal
January 26, 1914	February 13, 1915	Wood	Tiger
February 14, 1915	February 2, 1916	Wood	Rabbit
February 3, 1916	January 22, 1917	Fire	Dragon
January 23, 1917	February 10, 1918	Fire	Snake
February 11, 1918	January 31, 1919	Earth	Horse
February, 1, 1919	February 19, 1920	Earth	Goat
February 20, 1920	February 7, 1921	Metal	Monkey
February 8, 1921	January 27, 1922	Metal	Rooster
January 28, 1922	February 15, 1923	Water	Dog
February 16, 1923	February 4, 1924	Water	Pig
February 5, 1924	January 24, 1925	Wood	Rat
January 25, 1925	February 12, 1926	Wood	Ox
February 13, 1926	February 1, 1927	Fire	Tiger
February 2, 1927	January 22, 1928	Fire	Rabbit
January 23, 1928	February 9, 1929	Earth	Dragon
February 10, 1929	January 29, 1930	Earth	Snake
January 30, 1930	February 16, 1931	Metal	Horse
February 17, 1931	February 5, 1932	Metal	Goat
February 6, 1932	January 25, 1933	Water	Monkey
January 26, 1933	February 13, 1934	Water	Rooster
February 14, 1934	February 3, 1935	Wood	Dog
February 4, 1935	January 23, 1936	Wood	Pig
January 24, 1936	February 10, 1937	Fire	Rat
February 11, 1937	January 30, 1938	Fire	Ox
January 31, 1938	February 18, 1939	Earth	Tiger
February 19, 1939	February 7, 1940	Earth	Rabbit
February 8, 1940	January 26, 1941	Metal	Dragon
January 27, 1941	February 14, 1942	Metal	Snake
February 15, 1942	February 4, 1943	Water	Horse
February 5, 1943	January 24, 1944	Water	Goat
January 25, 1944	February 12, 1945	Wood	Monkey
February 13, 1945	February 1, 1946	Wood	Rooster

Find Your Chinese Birth Sign

From	To	Element	Animal
February 2, 1946	January 21, 1947	Fire	Dog
January 22, 1947	February 9, 1948	Fire	Pig
February 10, 1948	January 28, 1949	Earth	Rat
January 29, 1949	February 16, 1950	Earth	Ox
February 17, 1950	February 5, 1951	Metal	Tiger
February 6, 1951	January 26, 1952	Metal	Rabbit
January 27, 1952	February 13, 1953	Water	Dragon
February 14, 1953	February 2, 1954	Water	Snake
February 3, 1954	January 23, 1955	Wood	Horse
January 24, 1955	February 11, 1956	Wood	Goat
February 12, 1956	January 30, 1957	Fire	Monkey
January 31, 1957	February 17, 1958	Fire	Rooster
February 18, 1958	February 7, 1959	Earth	Dog
February 8, 1959	January 27, 1960	Earth	Pig
January 28, 1960	February 14, 1961	Metal	Rat
February 15, 1961	February 4, 1962	Metal	Ox
February 5, 1962	January 24, 1963	Water	Tiger
January 25, 1963	February 12, 1964	Water	Rabbit
February 13, 1964	February 1, 1965	Wood	Dragon
February 2, 1965	January 20, 1966	Wood	Snake
January 21, 1966	February 8, 1967	Fire	Horse
February 9, 1967	January 29, 1968	Fire	Goat
January 30, 1968	February 16, 1969	Earth	Monkey
February 17, 1969	February 5, 1970	Earth	Rooster
February 6, 1970	January 26, 1971	Metal	Dog
January 27, 1971	February 14, 1972	Metal	Pig
February 15, 1972	February 2, 1973	Water	Rat
February 3, 1973	January 22, 1974	Water	Ox
January 23, 1974	February 10, 1975	Wood	Tiger
February 11, 1975	January 30, 1976	Wood	Rabbit
January 31, 1976	February 17, 1977	Fire	Dragon
February 18, 1977	February 6, 1978	Fire	Snake
February 7, 1978	January 27, 1979	Earth	Horse

Find Your Chinese Birth Sign

From	To	Element	Animal
January 28, 1979	February 15, 1980	Earth	Goat
February 16, 1980	February 4, 1981	Metal	Monkey
February 5, 1981	January 24, 1982	Metal	Rooster
January 25, 1982	February 12, 1983	Water	Dog
February 13, 1983	February 1, 1984	Water	Pig
February 2, 1984	February 19, 1985	Wood	Rat
February 20, 1985	February 8, 1986	Wood	Ox
February 9, 1986	January 28, 1987	Fire	Tiger
January 29, 1987	February 16, 1988	Fire	Rabbit
February 17, 1988	February 5, 1989	Earth	Dragon
February 6, 1989	January 26, 1990	Earth	Snake
January 27, 1990	February 14, 1991	Metal	Horse
February 15, 1991	February 3, 1992	Metal	Goat
February 4, 1992	January 22, 1993	Water	Monkey
January 23, 1993	February 9, 1994	Water	Rooster
February 10, 1994	January 30, 1995	Wood	Dog
January 31, 1995	February 18, 1996	Wood	Pig
February 19, 1996	February 6, 1997	Fire	Rat
February 7, 1997	January 27, 1998	Fire	Ox
January 28, 1998	February 15, 1999	Earth	Tiger
February 16, 1999	February 4, 2000	Earth	Rabbit
February 5, 2000	January 23, 2001	Metal	Dragon
January 24, 2001	February 11, 2002	Metal	Snake
February 12, 2002	January 31, 2003	Water	Horse
February 1, 2003	January 21, 2004	Water	Goat
January 22, 2004	February 8, 2005	Wood	Monkey
February 9, 2005	January 28, 2006	Wood	Rooster
January 29, 2006	February 17, 2007	Fire	Dog
February 18, 2007	February 6, 2008	Fire	Pig
February 7, 2008	January 25, 2009	Earth	Rat
January 26, 2009	February 13, 2010	Earth	Ox
February 14, 2010	February 2, 2011	Metal	Tiger
February 3, 2011	January 22, 2012	Metal	Rabbit

Find Your Chinese Birth Sign

From	To	Element	Animal
January 23, 2012	February 9, 2013	Water	Dragon
February 10, 2013	January 30, 2014	Water	Snake
January 31, 2014	February 18, 2015	Wood	Horse
February 19, 2015	February 7, 2016	Wood	Goat
February 8, 2016	January 27, 2017	Fire	Monkey
January 28, 2017	February 15, 2018	Fire	Rooster
February 16, 2018	February 4, 2019	Earth	Dog
February 5, 2019	January 24, 2020	Earth	Pig

The Rat/Mouse

The Eclectic Rat (Tze)— the "Concealed Charmer"

January 31, 1900 to February 18, 1901: Metal Rat
February 18, 1912 to February 5, 1913: Water Rat
February 5, 1924 to January 24, 1925: Wood Rat
January 24, 1936 to February 10, 1937: Fire Rat
February 10, 1948 to January 28, 1949: Earth Rat
January 28, 1960 to February 14, 1961: Metal Rat
February 15, 1972 to February 2, 1973: Water Rat
February 2, 1984 to February 19, 1985: Wood Rat
February 19, 1996 to February 6, 1997: Fire Rat
February 7, 2008 to January 25, 2009: Earth Rat

Polarity: yang (positive)
Sign order: first
Alternate name: Mouse
Symbolism: infant, seed
Lucky color: midnight blue
Fragrance: sandalwood

Flavor: salty
Food/beverage: whole grains/dark ale
Flower: holly
Gem: turquoise
Feng shui direction: north
Lucky number: three

The first position in the Chinese Zodiac, the Rat, is one of charm, creativity, and survival. Those souls born into Rat years learn the lesson of "concealment," as an embryo is hidden within the womb. The Rat is analytical, always curious, and highly intelligent.

Rats inhabit a private world, one that is hidden from view and camouflaged—a place of retreat. They use charm to deflect and evade unpleasantness whenever possible. Under duress, Rats know how to take cover, artfully dodging both expectations and intrusions. Because they are always alert, Rats may seem anxious or nervous at times. Their attentiveness allow them to avoid many traps and dangers in life. The Rat represents fertility, the ability to live unseen, and intelligence. Being consumate suriviors, Rats have the ability to adapt easily to most circumstances.

Talkative and fascinating, the Rat is a natural in social situations, and is always a favorite party guest. However, the Rat is essentially introverted by nature and feels the most comfortable when socializing with close friends and family. Master of many trades, the eclectic Rat has an innate sense of human nature and is observant of those around them. According to Chinese folk legend, as maturity approaches, Rats are believed to acquire the gift of prophecy. They are natural teachers, and enjoy imparting life's knowledge to all who care to listen (often doing so well into the midnight hour).

The most harmonious time of day for the Rat is between 11 p.m. and 1 a.m., when the dark yin force reaches its peak. The stealthy Rat rules these arcane hours that encompass the yin and the yang. It is said that the Rat has a split personality because of this. In spite of their love of parties and sharing of nightly confidences, midnight should be a time of rest and regeneration for them.

Essential Temperament

Analytical and, at times, argumentative, the Rat will gain the upper hand in any verbal battle of wits. Worry (especially over health matters), excitability, and a quick temper can also be part of their nature.

Although lovable, the Rat is a bit of an opportunist. Most cannot resist making a good deal. Disarmingly charming and materialistic, this soul is warm-hearted, passionate, and wired to live for the moment.

Those born into Rat years are lovable and remain physically attractive throughout their lives. Rats are so resourceful and ambitious that they are often very financially successful. They love to acquire possessions and are extraordinarily good at spotting a bargain. An occasional Rat will become greedy or stingy, but most are kindhearted and fair. The perfect gift for a Rat person is an unusual object that has come from a faraway place, such as a relic from an ancient tomb.

Those born into Rat years are always in pursuit of a new adventure. Rats are natural explorers and voyagers. They adore all things different and unusual. Rats usually love to travel, and any foreign voyage will excite them. Favorite escape places for the Rat are caves, caverns, underground passages, and catacombs. Bizarre and forbidden places, such as abandoned castles and undiscovered ruins, fascinate the inquisitive Rat.

Verbally candid and agile, the Rat excels as a critic. The Rat lives by its wits and, given a choice, avoids manual labor (often directing others to get the task done). They prefer to use their brain to problem-solve and create adventures and possibilities. Rats also make excellent managers and business owners.

Rats have an unusually fruitful imagination and an insatiable thirst for knowledge. With a desire for diverse experiences, the Rat is a true magician of words and imagination. The season of the year when born, summer or winter, strongly influences the life of the Rat. Those born in the summer, when food is plentiful and grain lofts full, are less prone to worry. It is said that a Rat born in the winter must endlessly scavenge for food and will always fear poverty.

The Rat personality can be difficult to understand. It is intricate and occasionally contradictory. The effusive Rat can talk to anyone about anything. Although Rats are sharp critics, they usually maintain propriety and diplomacy. Rats are also amusing and entertaining companions, being both intellectually sharp and versatile. Fidgety and restless, Rats detest boring routine, and variety is what this soul seeks.

The Other Side—the Rat's Duality

In contrast to their many admirable attributes, unenlightened Rats can be covert, secretive, and will deflect or mislead if it is to their advantage. They are difficult to please, demanding, and highly critical of others. Often their standards are so unreasonable that they are impossible for others to uphold. Despite their surface composure, Rats may also be gnawed by a devastating feeling of insecurity. Due to their congeniality, Rats usually have an impressive circle of acquaintances at their fingertips, and an unscrupulous Rat will take full advantage of this. Profiteering and opportunistic behavior represents the Rat's energy being directed in its most unproductive form. It is for this reason that some Rats have difficulty making or keeping close friends. Expressed in its darkest form, this energy becomes dishonesty, agitation, restlessness, neurosis, aggressiveness, pettiness, hypochondria, and seclusion. The choice lies entirely with the individual. Taken to extreme, histrionic or avoidant personality disorders may develop.

Gifts and Capabilities

Being high-strung by nature, Rats hate alarm clocks, agendas, and pressure. They work most efficiently in solitary situations. Rat souls are rarely content working for others. This explains the surprising number of business owners, shopkeepers, and entrepreneurs who were born into Rat years. When Rats make money it is directly attributable to their acute intelligence.

Rats are the thriftiest souls in the Chinese Zodiac. Every expenditure is carefully considered, and all pennies spent are accounted for and justified. Rats worry about their financial future, and soberly consider every purchase or investment.

Many Rats possess a talent for writing, especially in the areas of fantasy, ancient lore, and science fiction. The Rat has an uncanny imagination, and many gifted writers and publicists were born in Rat years. Their imagination thrives in sequestered nooks, in worlds of their own, private and lost to view.

The deep-seated creativity of this sign cries out for expression either through writing, sculpture, or painting. Art reproductions, verbatim at times, are a Rat specialty. Expression through music is another way Rats channel their creative energies. This sign boasts many composers and conductors. The combination of imagination and depth can motivate the Rat to write a classic novel, compose a brilliant symphony, or acquire and sell the rarest of lost art treasures.

Those born under the sign of the Rat enjoy the material comforts of life. Food and housing are their highest priorities. Rats always stock up for a rainy day, feeling most comfortable with a little extra stored away. The Rat lives in the present and harbors fear of lack in the future. The Rat can feel isolated and tends to suffer alone. Money, or the lack thereof, is a particular concern. However, as a result of their cleverness and meticulous attention to detail, Rats usually make money rather easily. The Rat is an organizational genius at home and prefers a neat and tidy atmosphere.

The Child

As children, little Rats are sweet and loving, and have charming dispositions. However, like Monkey and Tiger children, Rat children are extremely hyperactive. They may seem shy, but inwardly Rat children are quite competitive. These little survivors are blessed with an accelerated metabolism, and even the most premature of Rat infants have a good chance for survival. This child will talk at an early age and take an interest in cooking and helping around the home. Being affectionate and demonstrative, this child will enjoy group play and will make friends easily. The highly intelligent Rat child will be an avid reader and will learn to use words early in life.

Home and Hearth

Rat parents like to teach and impart knowledge to their youngsters. The Rat is an alert parent who always makes sure their children have opportunities to learn, to experiment, and to understand. These parents will provide nutritious food that enhances children both mentally and physically. Rats are self-conscious and do not enjoy being the center of family photographs, home movies, or photo albums. The evasive nature of this sensitive soul does not like to feel exposed.

The most favorable time of year for cozy Rats is during the post-harvest winter months between late January and late February. At this time the storehouses are stocked with food and families are sequestered, safe, sheltered, and secure. Good food and good conversation can be shared and the Rat can enjoy the results of their labor.

Both male and female Rats are gregarious and tend to lead an extremely active social life. Wherever these talkative charmers find themselves, their presence is welcome. Rat souls liven up any reunion in which they take part. These souls love entertaining and do it with knowledge and refinement. Their guests, who are numerous, find them the most entertaining of hosts and hostesses and are inclined to lavish compliments on them.

Auspicious Careers

The best career choices for the Rat include salesperson, technical writer, art or film critic, business owner, pawnbroker or antique dealer, financial lender, politician, musician, philosopher, or scientist. Rats will also make excellent managers, bosses, and business owners.

Many journalists and writers are found under this sign. In addition, some of the most successful salesmen and women are Rats. Commercial traveler, legal or financial expert, and broker are also natural career choices for the Rat. Forensic pathologist, criminologist, detective, and even undercover spy work can also be a good fit.

The Famous and the Infamous

Some well-known Rats include: Antonio Banderas, Hugh Grant, Ozzy Osbourne, David Duchovny, Alan Alda, Samuel L. Jackson, Al Gore, Sarah Vaughan, Joan Jett, Vanessa Redgrave, Daryl Hannah, Richard Simmons, Howard Dean, Gwyneth Paltrow, Sean Penn, Cameron Diaz, William Shakespeare, Leo Tolstoy, Jules Verne, Charlotte Bronte, Truman Capote, T.S. Eliot, Eugene O'Neill, Margaret Mitchell, Racine, George Sand, Defoe, Jules Renard, Toulouse-Lautrec, Amadeus Mozart, Louis Armstrong, Irving Berlin, Joseph Hayden, Zubin Mehta, Aaron Copeland, T.S. Eliot, Claude Monet, Prince Charles, and Presidents George Washington and Franklin Pierce.

Summary

Sweet Rat, you so need a sympathetic ear and a soft place to fall. It's all right to relax those rigid standards of yours and ask for what you need. Never view yourself as a jack-of-all-trades and master of none. You draw your knowledge from a wide variety of sources, which is an art unto itself. Let go of your perfectionist ways; no melon is completely round and no person is perfect. As an oil lamp becomes brighter after trimming, your truth will always become clearer after being discussed. So, let's talk.

Call the keeper of dreams.
I would claim mine now.
No longer will the shackles
Of spent yesterdays
Or the yoke of unknown tomorrows
Restrain me.
I am set free
By the power found in loving me.
Call the keeper of dreams.
I would claim mine now.

The Rat Woman

Jan is an organizational genius. She also holds the title of the thriftiest woman in her family. Each purchase she makes and every penny she spends will have a useful and well-considered purpose. Despite having a handsome trust account and a steady income, Jan worries about her financial future. Her sharp eye for detail gives her a distinct advantage both professionally and personally, but she is not made for hard physical work. Her fortunate financial position can be attributed to her acute intelligence, rather than to the sweat of her brow.

Her company is the kind people eagerly seek. Sincere, direct, and highly intelligent, others appreciate her efficiency, her scrutiny, and her dependability. However, Jan's positive qualities constitute only one part of her complicated personality. When her defenses are down, Jan suffers from many compulsions and obsessions. She feels uneasy in her human frailty and is convinced that there is always something that she should be "doing." Psychologically and emotionally delicate, Jan is on a life quest for her personal identity. Confidentially, she will admit that her greatest fear is of being alone. Dependent on a significant other, she is a soul who frankly cannot be isolated or stranded on an emotional beach.

She will be the first to admit that she is not easy to live with. This is a woman who needs to hold her husband in high esteem. She has fixed opinions and has difficulty compromising these. Her husband's arguments are mute points that she effusively rebuts item by item. However, Jan is unquestionably an outstanding mother. She goes out of her way to be a friend to her children and relishes their confidences. She intends to nurture their talents and increase their intelligence. Being a mother brings her a feeling of comfort and reassurance.

Kimmy's big, brown eyes and cute-as-a-button charm conceal a cunning and upwardly mobile young woman. Underneath her pixie exterior resides a lucid mind and a superbly sarcastic wit. Kimmy's feminine and dainty appearance masks a resourceful, intelligent, and practical woman. Her charming personality and natural interest in writing and literature have allowed her to become a highly successful publicist. She is invaluable to her author clients in making contacts and persuading publishers. Journalism, literary pursuits, and the entertainment industry are natural fields for her, and her dream is to become a television or radio personality. Her competence is well-recognized. However, she lacks self-confidence, and is plagued by various emotional problems. Teamwork suits her well, as do positions that provide strong moral support.

Kimmy's health, like many Rat women, is delicate. She is highly sensitive to spores, pollen, animal dander, and other allergens. Sinusitis and bronchitis have become less bothersome as middle age has approached, but still cause her to suffer. Her emotional health has improved through experience and maturity, which has resulted in greater self-confidence.

Both Jan and Kimmy love the nightlife and seldom miss an opportunity to socialize. When relaxed and at ease, they are soft-spoken, well-mannered, discreet, and never at a loss for words. Both ladies are excellent conversationalists and diplomatic concerning sensitive issues. This diplomacy has mitigated many delicate and awkward situations. However, if feeling antagonistic, Jan and Kimmy (as is the case with their other Rat sisters) have the mental and verbal skills to launch a full-blown assault, replete with shocking statements and sarcastic barbs.

For example, Kimmy's need for perfection can quickly work her up to a nervous fever pitch, at which time her friendly demeanor disintegrates. Unable to restore her composure once stresses have gone beyond a certain point, Kimmy has said things in anger that she regrets.

After the storm clouds have cleared, each lady returns to her amusing, kind, witty, and warm persona. Each is cherished for their adaptability, organization, and ability to deal with countless precarious situations.

The Rat Man

Whether tinkering with a new hobby or researching the details on an obscure scientific phenomenon, Tim leaves no stone unturned. He aims to do things correctly, or not at all. But, like his Tiger brothers, today's passion is not necessarily tomorrow's pursuit. Tim becomes an instant expert on any subject he tackles, and his "projects" can turn his humble home into a mad professor's laboratory. Highly intelligent and curious, Tim excels at exhaustingly dissecting and reproducing scientific and artistic phenomena.

At any one time, Tim may be designing a new type of harpsichord key or a homemade ionic air purifier. His office (and irked wife's kitchen) is strewn with Tim's latest projects. This month it is a "perpetual motion device" run only by magnets that has Tim enthralled. He would love nothing more than to have the local energy company buy his unique solar panel design (which takes up most of his irked wife's patio). Tim is also a gifted musician. Despite his boundless talent, he rarely plays or composes anymore, because he feels that he could never be "the best." His desire for perfection shadows him in chronic malaise.

Ron has been a technical writer for 30 years. He is a genius at writing and illustrating complex technical manuals for the aerospace industry with precision and scrutiny. Seldom calling in sick and *never* late for work, Ron's personal life is similarly ordered. His home is always neat and tidy and Ron's family looks forward to his lavish gourmet cooking.

Despite his technical writing capabilities, Ron is a romantic. He has an elaborate body of work that few know about or have ever seen. He dreams of writing a matchless science-fiction or extraordinary novel alive with fantasy and legends. Ron is in good company, sharing his taste and sensitivity with his literary Rat brothers William Shakespeare, Leo Tolstoy, Daniel Defoe, and Jules Verne.

Ron was a strikingly handsome young man, and at the age of 60 he looks no more than 45. Always scrupulous regarding his outward appearance, Ron moves with grace and continues to remain youthful.

Both Tim and Ron enjoy good physical health. However, their digestive systems are touchy, and they each suffer from heartburn and indigestion. In addition, Tim has suffered with various nervous conditions, from hyperactivity as a child, to emotional volitility in his early adult years. Both men have sensitive nervous systems, and each must be cautious regarding high blood pressure and cardiac health.

In social situations where they feel accepted and admired, both Tim and Ron are charming, talkative, and all-around delightful men. However, both men hold their cards close to their chest. Their essence of "concealment" causes them to keep many secrets and disguise their true motives.

Effusive and helpful when times are good, during a crisis Rats are fragile and withdraw deep inside their private mental nooks. While deeply family-oriented and attached, Rat men struggle with fidelity. This is not to say that all Rat males are philanderers, only that their insatiable curiosity and search for diversity can cause them conflicts. Rat men can also take their spouses for granted, becoming emotionally engaged only when there is trouble in paradise.

As fathers, both men are excellent providers but keep a subconscious distance from their children. Only upon reestablishing a new relationship of peer-quality with an older child do Rats reap the rich rewards of parenthood. Rat men adore babies and are tender and almost maternally nurturing towards infants. However, as the children become a little older, the Rat male falls apart, so to speak, at maintaining this closeness. Like their Rabbit bothers, Rat men isolate themselves and detach from their offspring during the grammar and junior high school years, only to become as close as a best friend when the children reach adulthood. It is then that this detached, busy, perfectionist negotiates a close and involved relationship with their child.

Both Tim and Ron fiercely hold on to the fallacy that they are "jack of all trades and masters of none." This self-effacing thinking casts a cloud over the joy they should rightly feel with their accomplishments.

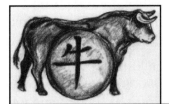

The Ox

The Durable Ox (Chou)— the "Head Honcho"

February 19, 1901 to February 7, 1902: Metal Ox
February 6, 1913 to January 25, 1914: Water Ox
January 25, 1925 to February 12, 1926: Wood Ox
February 11, 1937 to January 30, 1938: Fire Ox
January 29, 1949 to February 16, 1950: Earth Ox
February 15, 1961 to February 4, 1962: Metal Ox
February 3, 1973 to January 22, 1974: Water Ox
February 20, 1985 to February 8, 1986: Wood Ox
February 7, 1997 to January 27, 1998: Fire Ox
January 26, 2009 to February 13, 2010: Earth Ox

Polarity: yin (negative)
Sign order: second
Alternate name: Buffalo
Symbolism: nurturing
   parent
Lucky color: forest green
Fragrance: frankincense

Flavor: sweet
Food/beverage: yeast
   breads/tea, coffee
Flower: carnation
Gem: lapis lazuli
Feng shui direction:
   north-northeast
Lucky number: one

The second position in the Chinese Zodiac, the Ox, is one of strength and perseverance. Those souls born into Ox years learn the lesson of "endurance," possessing strength of the abundant, earthy, yin variety. In China, the Ox is the symbol of parental love because of the tenderness with which the Ox nurtures its calf. Oxen are deeply devoted to their children and families, and possess a quiet and un-complaining strength. Home and the earth are the two great sources of the Oxen's legendary perseverance and stability.

Smart and responsible, stable and dedicated, Oxen walk the straight and narrow paths in life. They are conservative to a fault and express themselves powerfully and convincingly, commanding the respect of others. The sharp mind of the Ox, combined with this natural elo-quence of speech, makes them credible and patriotic leaders. Natives of Ox years are often called to high office. Eager and conquering, and possessing an iron will, they prove formidable crusaders in life.

Many Oxen will find success through public speaking, the enter-tainment business, or politics. Possessing an inborn authority and strong determination, Oxen triumph in life through sheer stubborn-ness. Ox-year souls are tenacious by nature and can survive incred-ible adversity. This capacity to endure, even through great hardships, has kept whole nations and families together. Oxen possess practical, down-to-earth advice, and are more competent than most.

The most harmonious time of each day for the Ox is between 1 a.m. and 3 a.m., the peaceful early morning hours. This is when the endur-ing Ox rests and assembles the strength to push past the obstacles of the coming day. According to Chinese tradition, those born into Ox years will be happier if born in the winter, as there is less work to do in the fields. An Ox born in the summer is fated to work harder throughout their life.

Essential Temperament

Sober-minded Oxen know the value of doing things correctly. These personalities are truly grounded and not easily swayed. This is the patient "marathon" personality of the Zodiac, as opposed to the mercurial "sprint" temperament characteristic of some of the other signs.

People born into Ox years require contact with nature. They find solace in tending and planting their gardens, landscaping beautiful homes, and working the land. Oxen are known for their "green thumbs" and are often accomplished gardeners, agriculturists, or involved in the buying and selling of real estate.

Some favorite places for the Ox are tranquil meadows, quiet ponds, and secluded spots unknown to others. The earthy Ox also nurtures and protects the small, the weak, and the helpless, thereby representing the goddess of mercy, Kwan Yin, and the sacredness of life.

The Other Side—the Ox's Duality

In contrast to their many admirable attributes, unenlightened Oxen can be overly stern, display terrible tempers, and be so rigid as to become immovable (even when the facts prove otherwise). An Ox hates being contradicted, especially in front of others, and can be subject to extreme outbreaks of anger like the proverbial "bull in a china shop." One is advised to steer clear until the calm emerges from the storm. Oxen do not enjoy being teased, and possess a choleric temperament. Oxen also dislike insubordination, defiance, and disloyalty of any kind, and are capable of holding grudges for long durations. Authoritarianism and extreme rigidity represent the Ox's energy being directed in a most unproductive form. Expressed in its darkest form, this energy becomes possessiveness, brooding, stubbornness, lack of empathy, resistance to movement, jealousy, and revenge. The choice lies entirely with the individual. Taken to an extreme, antisocial or narcissistic personality disorders may develop.

Gifts and Capabilities

Oxen are the most dependable, patient, composed, and tireless workers of the Chinese Zodiac. Laziness and idleness are abhorrent to the average Ox. Once set on a goal, Oxen work hard to complete their tasks. Conservative, traditional, and dutiful, Oxen take on projects that others do not have the patience to complete. Physical exhaustion must be guarded against, as Oxen reliably practice the Chinese proverb of "sow much, reap much; sow little, reap little." The health of those born into Ox years is generally good. Of a sturdy constitution, they are blessed with great longevity, but must guard against settling into a sedentary lifestyle.

Outdoor activities such as gardening or building are good sources of physical exercise for the Ox. Some stomach or intestinal problems, as well as complications from overindulgence in drinking, smoking, or an unhealthy diet could be experienced from time to time. The Ox is also susceptible to environmental and climactic changes. It is advisable for them to avoid extremes of hot or cold weather. Male Oxen are cautioned to guard against obesity; females should be aware of gynecological disorders or hormonal imbalances.

Patient, persistent, and persevering, the most difficult obstacle for the Ox to overcome is their inability to understand those who are different from themselves. The Ox is precise and methodical, and their best roles are those of ethical mediator, moral judge, or negotiator.

The Child

As a baby and child, little Oxen are the most enduring and physically resilient members of the family. Don't try to bend the rules or sneak something past this tot, as you will be caught and corrected. The Ox child is opinionated and serious in life. Parents need to encourage the Ox child's sense of humor and lighten this private little person's load a bit. Gifted with their hands, these lovable little dictators are more comfortable with the familiar and consistent. This child needs a regular routine and prefers meals served at the family table with all in attendance and on time. This stoic child is not whiny or teary, but rather strong and helpful. They also may need some prodding to open up and have more fun in life. An Ox child is physically strong, and Oxen of both sexes are the luckiest children when it comes to surviving physically traumatic injuries. This child leaves the frivolities and fast talk to other kids. They have a firm sense of self and tend to follow few.

Home and Hearth

Duty, family obligations, and physical comforts play important roles in the daily existence of those born under this sign. The Ox has a serious nature and is blessed with natural composure and presence of mind. They are family-oriented. As parents, Oxen want their children to be obedient. Oxen parents lavish much affection, practical care, and self-sacrifice on their children. They handle child-rearing chores as they do all other work, correctly and efficiently. Ox parents are indeed the earth mothers and fathers of the world. Regarding both children and animals (Oxen dearly love them both), a balanced combination of firmness and love are applied.

The most favorable time of year for the persevering Ox is between late February and early March. This is the time when all life slowly reawakens and Oxen are renewed with energy, new stamina, and romantic desires.

The Ox craves peace, stability, and a beautiful place to live. An Oxen's home is unmistakably their castle, and Ox houses are cozy and well organized. Due to the Oxen's love of the earth, favorite family activities are planting, fishing, or just taking in the view. Oxen enjoy quiet, private places to unwind. Although fully capable of taking on the outside world, the Ox will be happiest organizing and taking care of their home. Men and women alike will thrive incorporating outside work into a home-based business. Being self-motivated and productive souls, the well-disciplined, solitary Ox works best independently.

Auspicious Careers

Oxen are talented and skilled with their hands. Gifted in any art of touch or craft, tactile Oxen are often craftsmen, painters, artisans, farmers, gourmet cooks, expert seamstresses, quilters, and skillful musicians. Oxen feel the need to touch, toy with, and dabble dexterously with the world around them. The best career choices for someone born into an Ox year are those professions performed alone. Many are statesmen, military strategists, surgeons, veterinarians, dictators, police officers, architects, archaeologists, farmers, elementary teachers, gourmet cooks, and public speakers. Whatever the career, Oxen prefer either to be the boss or to work alone.

The Famous and the Infamous

Performers, war leaders, dictators, and even princesses find themselves born under the sign of the Ox. Famous Oxen include: George Clooney, Jack Nicholson, Princess Diana of Wales, Meg Ryan, Bill Cosby, Bill O'Reilly, Sean Hannity, Neve Campbell, Jim Carrey, Sigourney Weaver, Michael Richards, Kate Moss, Meryl Streep, Melissa Etheridge, Anthony Hopkins, Napoleon, Idi Amin, Malcolm X, Geronimo, Saddam Hussein, Adolph Hitler, Lafayette, Nehru, Richard the Lion-heart, the Marquise de Pompadour, Aristotle, Robert Kennedy, Charlie Chaplin, Dante, Renoir, Johann Sebastian Bach, George Frederic Handel, Walt Disney, Bruce Springsteen, Clark Gable, Peter Sellers, Richard Burton, Hans Christian Andersen, Richard and Pat Nixon, Gerald Ford, Gore Vidal, Art Buchwald, Johnny Carson, Sammy Davis Jr., Jane Fonda, Angela Lansbury, William Buckley, Colin Powell, and Margaret Thatcher.

Summary

Patient Ox, you tend to isolate yourself and take life much too seriously. All work and no play does indeed accomplish your goals, but at what price? Your sense of duty is admirable, but let others carry some of the load. A single thread can't make a cord, or a single tree a forest. The most precious gift you can give others is a relaxed and balanced *you*. Our actions reflect our intentions, and yours are above reproach. However, a knife will rust if not sharpened regularly and water will stagnate if it is not allowed to flow. Embrace new ideas and do not fear change. Now, go plant that beautiful garden of yours.

The mantle
Of responsibility
Weighs heavily
Upon your shoulders.
Your granite world
Demands a stoic strength.
Rest now,
And share with me your dreams
Of untilled meadows.

The Ox Woman

Karen's style is simple and practical. She runs her home with the efficiency of a four-star general. Blessed with a level head and good manners, others consider her humorous, communicative, and easy to be with. Karen is also an extraordinary cook and firmly believes that "food is life, and life is love."

Graced with a down-to-earth approach to life, she cares little for the latest trends in fashion and feels most comfortable in casual cottons and classic styles. Karen enjoys good physical health and a robust endurance. However, endocrine and gynecological problems have caused her trouble throughout her childbearing years.

When times are good and life is on the upswing, Karen is a sincere and straightforward woman. She is busy, talkative, cheerful, and a most enjoyable companion. Nevertheless, her fine sense of humor quickly disintegrates when the order and efficiency of her home is threatened or if her authority is challenged.

Another way to wave a red flag in front of this proud lady is to insult or show disrespect for past traditions, family history, or anything related to her childhood and parents. Similar to her Dog sister, Karen's family is of highest priority and she is capable of doing anything and everything to protect the members of her inner circle. She holds dear the morals and teachings of her youth and she stubbornly refuses to change her established habits. Karen is most comfortable with the familiar and conventional ways of life.

Like Karen, Joanne is an extremely hard worker. Nothing irritates her more than inactivity or laziness. Maintaining financial security and providing the good things in life for her family allows her to sleep well at night. But despite her many sterling qualities, Joanne is headstrong and supremely stubborn. Once she has made up her mind, she holds on to her decision with a death-grip. She can usually be persuaded with sentimentality, and she is quite tender when it comes to matters of the heart. However, hers is a soul that must be in charge. Criticism, disrespect, and insubordination arouse her fury.

Constant, dependable, and circumspect, Joanne is invaluable to her husband's business. She organizes the shop efficiently and balances the books with amazing accuracy. She thrives in this flexible environment that allows her the freedom to also care for her home and children. Joanne, as do most Oxen, has her roots in the earth itself, and she is seldom happier than when pruning her spectacular rose garden, planting her annual vegetables, or nurturing her various pets.

Joanne has a green thumb, and her home resembles a small forest of lush houseplants and fresh-cut flowers. Her supreme patience allows her to produce fine crafts of every type. Her hands are never idle, whether knitting, crocheting, embroidering, or finishing the details on a custom quilt, routine does not deter her. Each painstaking stitch brings her closer to a finished masterpiece.

Her talent for exacting and difficult tasks makes her a welcome addition to any work team, and her nurturing nature opens up a plethora of vocational possibilities. Karen, like her Ox sister, Princess Diana of Wales, loves children. She blooms as she walks into her morning kindergarten class and the children run to greet her.

Karen was a late starter romantically. And while she would love nothing more than to have her own children someday, she will admit that she is quite happy being self-sufficient. She would welcome, but does not need, a husband to complete her. Being deeply conservative, unless Karen finds the man of her dreams and marries, it is unlikely that she will have her own children.

Comfortable and content with themselves, both Karen and Joanne are vigilant and practical Ox women. Affectionate and nurturing, they are loved (and respected) by all those who call them "friend."

The Ox Man

Tyler is the epitome of firmness and stability. He possesses the soul of a great sequoia redwood tree, standing tall and enduring through time and the elements. Despite his young age, Tyler is a man well grounded in his principles, firm in his convictions, and eminently patient as he pursues his goals.

Foresight and common sense move him cautiously forward in life and Tyler sensibly sticks to tried and traditional methods, rarely taking foolish risks. He thinks in terms of the concrete and the tangible. He knows where he is going in life and is prepared to tirelessly pursue his dreams. Like his Oxen sisters, Tyler is gifted with manual dexterity and expresses this talent as a musician.

Empowered and confident, Tyler has an answer to everything, and can be exasperatingly opinionated. Once convinced of a path, little can distract or change his chosen course. When obstacles stand in his way, he bulldozes past them. Tenacity and perseverance are his finest qualities, but rigidity and close-mindedness are also a part of his personality.

Usually calm and placid, Tyler rarely loses his temper. But when this young ox sees red, his fury explodes with authority. He gives new meaning to "walking softly and carrying a big stick." Like his Dog mother, Tyler's memory is long when it comes to ill treatment or disloyalty. His heart is a tender one, and emotional pain being unbearable, it is unconsciously transformed to anger.

Traditional and family-oriented, Greg cherishes the values of his parents and ancestors. He possesses a strong sense of loyalty toward his wife and children and responsibly provides for his aging parents. Second to his family, Greg's greatest passion is his work. He works hard and never accepts incomplete or shoddy outcomes. He is demanding, methodical, and will not accept failure.

Greg's needs are simple; his wants modest. This is a man who enjoys the fundamental things in life. Underling his sedate demeanor is an affectionate, deeply conscientious soul. Greg has no difficulty sorting out predicaments and judiciously separating petty problems from those of real importance. Like Tyler, Greg is cautious and does not open his heart nor give his loyalty freely. As a "marathon" soul, he requires time and proven performance in order to trust or become emotionally attached. However, once committed, whether to a friendship, employer, or spouse, it is everlasting. His sense of duty and responsibility are the most profound features of his psychological core. Those who know him well understand that he is awkward at expressing his emotions, preferring to demonstrate his devotion in practical and sensible ways.

Having a gift for leadership, Greg inspires others with his concrete thinking and confidence in his own convictions. He delights his wife with handmade furniture, various household crafts, and blue ribbon-winning tomatoes from his garden. As "earthy" as they come, Greg is not only a shrewd businessman, but a closet artist as well. On his own time he expresses himself in oil paintings, demonstrating creative dexterity with his hands. This is a soul who requires stability and order in his life. His home life is the key to his emotional happiness. A loving family, bountiful feasts, and loyal pet by his side will fill his heart.

Greg is a man who keeps a low profile and rarely calls attention to himself. He is never in a hurry and takes his time with everything he does. His quiet and unassuming manner, sparing words, and introspective demeanor can be misleading; when he speaks his well-thought-out words are persuasive and imposing.

Both Tyler and Greg find it difficult to accept advice from others, and prefer to give it rather than take it. Neither have any patience for foolish notions, nor sympathy for those who leap before they look. Both of these men trust only their own assessments, tend to be loners, and cherish just a few well-trusted friends. Endowed with superb organizational abilities, these firmly planted Ox men can also be harsh, if not downright ruthless, toward those who oppose or compete with them. The type of authority they possess is of karmic proportions.

Chapter 5

The Tiger

The Noble Tiger (Yin)— the "Go-Getter"

February 8, 1902 to January 28, 1903: Water Tiger
January 26, 1914 to February 13, 1915: Wood Tiger
February 13, 1926 to February 1, 1927: Fire Tiger
January 31, 1938 to February 18, 1939: Earth Tiger
February 17, 1950 to February 5, 1951: Metal Tiger
February 5, 1952 to January 24, 1963: Water Tiger
January 23, 1974 to February 10, 1975: Wood Tiger
February 9, 1986 to January 28, 1987: Fire Tiger
January 28, 1998 to February 15, 1999: Earth Tiger
February 14, 2010 to February 2, 2011: Metal Tiger

Polarity: yang (positive)
Sign order: third
Symbolism: military salute
Lucky color: purple
Fragrance: citrus
Flavor: sour

Food/beverage: poultry, carbonated sodas
Flower: violet
Gem: amethyst
Feng shui direction: east-northeast
Lucky number: seven

The third position in the Chinese Zodiac, the Tiger, is captivating, extreme, and rebellious. Those souls born into Tiger years learn the lesson of "nobility," and are symbolized by the respectful salute of honor from a subordinate to their leader. This classic "hero" type of personality represents power, courage, and action without forethought.

The Tiger plays for stakes and aims to win at the game of life. The competitive and self-assured Tiger seeks challenges and audience approval, and is fiercely independent. This fiercely self-reliant soul may appear gruff and tough on the outside, yet they are tenderhearted and affectionate toward those whom they love.

Because the Tiger is an animal of the yang disposition, it is their nature to be energetic, confident, and to end up in first place. The three unrivaled qualities of those born into Tiger years are courage, enthusiasm, and protectiveness. Tigers condemn shallow displays of sincerity, meddling, and all forms of personal criticism.

The most harmonious time of each day for the Tiger is between 3 a.m. and 5 a.m. These are the predawn hours when the yang force grows, and during which the Tiger refuels their endless energy and unfailing self-confidence. Little distinction exists between the genders of this sign. Both are graced with a strong character and great powers of resistance. Whether male or female, their immense energy allows Tigers to undertake sizable projects.

Essential Temperament

Tigers are engaging and dramatic companions who reject the mundane, preferring to search out the challenges and conquests in life. Tigers love to tempt fate and are always ready to set out on a new adventure or project. Legend states that the Tiger has the ability to appear and disappear at will. Tigers can be secretive, stealthily walking a tightrope between life and death.

The pleasure-loving Tiger enjoys attending parties and socializing, and is the most charming and spirited of hosts. Eager to please, lively, and gregarious, Tigers have a special personal aura and magnetism that entices others. Tigers love the unforeseen and they adore wandering about at random without knowing what to expect. They tempt fate, take chances, and fight for noble ideals.

Tigers are naturally empowered with a sense of superiority and permission to pass through life. They possess a natural attitude of "empowered entitlement" in their thinking; they also display unwavering courage, leadership, and visionary plans of action. The Tiger's wisdom provides willpower in the face of adversity and the ability to act in a timely manner.

The fields of endeavor that appeal most to Tigers are the ones that allow them to protest and fight for the rights of the ostracized. Tigers tend to be dissatisfied with the existing state of things and need to flex their muscles from time to time. Politics may fascinate the Tiger until they discover that it is a dirty game; they will then abandon this field because Tigers are nobly honest and offended by self-interest. The Tiger must pursue a career that offers sufficient dignity and challenge.

The Other Side—the Tiger's Duality

In contrast to their many admirable attributes, unenlightened Tigers can be careless, obstinate, rebellious, and undisciplined. Recklessness and hasty action without analysis represent the Tiger's energy being directed in a most unproductive form. Expressed in its darkest form, this energy becomes rebellion to the point of mutiny, outward toughness, boorishness, excessive envy, haste, bossiness, and imprudent thrill-seeking to the point of injury. The choice lies entirely with the individual. Taken to extreme, antisocial or oppositional/defiant personality disorders may develop.

Gifts and Capabilities

Tigers are playful, adventurous in the extreme, and always courageous. They are also deeply sensitive and public-spirited. Here one finds a soul who will always stand with friends and family during hard times. During a crisis, a Tiger will travel long and far to reach a loved one in trouble. According to Chinese legend, once provoked to rage, the Tigers are so fierce that only someone who does not care whether they live or die can combat them.

The humanitarian Tiger is thought to be protective and lucky, fending off the three main disasters of a household: fire, thieves, and evil spirits (Sha Chi.). To live with a Tiger is to jump into their domain of activity. Their dynamic personality takes over their world. There is a kingly, majestic aura surrounding Tigers, and they tend to be "bigger than life" in all endeavors. They are usually in a hurry and others have difficulty keeping up with them. Whether in the role of dynamic zealot or fearless pioneer, Tigers detest halfhearted efforts.

Travel is many times a favorite leisure activity. Exotic getaways where tourists are rare suit the Tiger well. Safaris, adventurous excursions, record-breaking mountain climbs, and sports records keep the brave Tiger youthful and healthy well into middle age. Caution regarding physical exhaustion must be exercised and Tigers must take time out for rest and relaxation.

Although loyal and generous, Tigers prefer to be in charge and never remain long in a subordinate position. Tigers have little tolerance for foolishness or incompetence and can be rash when revolting against authority and superiors. Boredom will sap the life from a Tiger; therefore, yesterday's occupation is not usually today's passion. Tigers are well known for their frequent job changes and for numerous changes of residence.

The Child

Tiger children are little dynamos and frequent visitors to the emergency room for various injuries. Due to the immense energy and risk-taking behavior of Tiger children, they have more than their share of childhood accidents. This is not an easy child to rear and there will be trouble at times.

Rebellious and demanding, busy Tiger children resist bedtimes and other schedule restrictions. They need large amounts of affection combined with firm limits. Patience with, and investments in, Tiger offspring are worth every gray hair. Most will bring great pride to their families through celebrated accomplishments in life.

Home and Hearth

Naturally an adventurer and conqueror, all Tigers are heads of their households. Tiger parents sincerely attempt to instill concepts of moderation and virtue, but may have trouble practicing what they preach to their offspring. A disciplined Tiger is an inspiring influence on their offspring, allowing them to seek excitement and encouraging them to expand their horizons. Tigers can also be overbearing with their youngsters and caution must be exercised with children who are hypersensitive or who hate to be rushed (Snakes, Pigs, and Rats).

The most favorable time of year for the Tiger is mid-March to mid-April, when new life has emerged and is in full bloom. The sensual Tiger comes alive with the tranquilizing perfume of spring.

Tigers love to entertain, and do so with flair. They make witty and boisterous conversation and serve lavish meals, asking nothing more than to be the center of attention.

Auspicious Careers

The Tiger favors anything in which they have a leadership role. If not bored, the Tiger will have a chance to advance further. The Tiger was born to be in charge. They do not like to take orders and excel at being the boss. The Tiger is creative and destructive, offensive and defensive. This trait can be used to run several different careers or businesses at one time. Although lucky and competent in making money, Tigers find that it slips easily through their paws. Enjoyment and comfort, not saving for a rainy day, are the Tiger's main objectives.

Many Tigers are performers, actors, singers, and musicians. Tigers are also found in unusual and sometimes dangerous occupations, including matadors, chief driver on a racing team, stuntperson, world explorer, military head, revolutionary, or mercenary. The natural role for a Tiger is that of commander-in-chief. The most dismal positions for Tigers are those of a servant or lower subject.

The Famous and the Infamous

Some famous and infamous Tigers include: Steve Irwin, Tom Cruise, Demi Moore, Rosie O'Donnell, Leonardo DiCaprio, Jodie Foster, Mel Brooks, John Corbett, Martin Short, Rush Limbaugh, Paula Abdul, Stevie Wonder, Garth Brooks, Phil Collins, Enya, Elliot Gould, Ludwig van Beethoven, Charles de Gaulle, Bo Gritz, Ho Chi Minh, Dwight D. Eisenhower, Karl Marx, Princess Anne, Sun Yat-sen, Will Geer, Alec Guinness, Queen Elizabeth II, Hugh Hefner, Marilyn Monroe, Natalie Wood, Emily Bronte, Elizabeth Barrett Browning, Isadora Duncan, Rudolph Nureyev, John Steinbeck, Oscar Wilde, Jean Kirkpatrick, Germaine Greer, and Peter Gabriel.

Summary

Brave Tiger, a little error can lead to a large discrepancy. Slow down and think matters through. Remember that "provisions should be arranged before an army is mobilized." Proper preparations should occur in advance to ensure success. Your gift of action without forethought serves you well if working as a paramedic or on the front lines of a battlefield. However, impulsive actions have a way of coming back to haunt you (not to mention putting you in traction). The squeaky wheels get the oil. The strong are expected to be strong. I know it's not fair, but it is your reality. Share your burdens with others—this does not compromise your independence. Confide your sorrows as well as triumphs to a loyal Dog, a cheerful Horse, or an honest Pig.

You have been given strong wings
That you might fly to the highest pinnacles
Of this life,
And a clear, keen eye
To behold the farthest horizons
Of your dreams.
The sheltered cliff of fear
Cannot hold you.
You shall soar on roaring winds of change
In splendid flight.

The Tiger Woman

Activity is a way of life for Cindy. Whether organizing the masses in a walk for charity or pushing past roadblocks into a forest fire—Cindy will be leading the way. Always the "alpha" female, Cindy walks fast, thinks fast, and works fast. She is in a perpetual state of movement. Impulsive and abrupt, she expresses herself eloquently albeit brashly at times. Few women are as loyal and capable as this young dynamo, and she is blessed with great courage and a sanguine temperament. Once set on a goal, she will zealously pursue a successful completion. Her ability to make quick assessments and immediate decisions makes her a natural for positions of authority.

Cindy's inexhaustible drive allows her to embark upon colossal projects and push her endurance to its limits. Exhaustion is usually at the core of her health problems and, being a woman of extremes, it is a daunting task to slow her down. Her driving attitude toward life and refusal to show weakness make it difficult for her to ask for help. Cindy is also a deeply emotional woman who responds fervently to situations and events that touch her heart. Despite her chaotic schedule, she always finds time for her aged parents. Her father, also a Tiger, is her role model and is a man of distinguished valor. His noble work ethic and heart "as big as a house" has, in large part, shaped Cindy's own character.

Like her father, others depend and lean on Cindy sometimes too heavily. Even this most independent of souls needs to be cared for and nurtured herself. Privately, she will confess that "the strong, are expected to always be strong" and that she resents the "squeaky wheels" who whine to get the oil. Tough on the outside, others seldom know how deeply wounded she can be by disloyalty, neglect, or apathy.

Tall, beautiful, and blessed with extraordinary charisma, Cindy is a hard worker and despises laziness. She considers herself totally equal to her husband (and to all men in general, for that matter). Humanitarian and optimistic, this is a soul who follows her own drummer and seeks causes and people worth sacrificing for. Her word is as good as gold and her profound loyalty is equal to none.

Painfully, like many Tiger women, Cindy has suffered with various hormonal, gynecological, and reproductive problems over the years. After a hysterectomy left her unable to have further children, she refused to retreat into depression or a full-fledged "pity party." She rebounded by organizing a large children's choir and is currently director of a summer camp for disabled children. Now she has many "babies" to tend, to teach, and to inspire.

On her own since the young age of 13, Nana's predominant weakness is her pride. She is self-taught and has no patience with those who complain or pretend to be helpless. Nana's father lost everything in the devastating "dust bowl" of the 1920s, which left her family destitute. She married the boy down the street just before her 13th birthday and took in her brothers and sisters to care for. In addition, she gave birth to her own child nine months later. Early on, Nana assumed important responsibilities. Her Tiger year of birth blessed her with the qualities she needed to survive, to lead, and to protect others. Many years, dramas, and grandchildren later, Nana commands the respect of both friends and foes.

Both Cindy and Nana have two predestined characteristics: Passion and protectiveness. As Tiger women they are fated to serve as the "empress" with the rest of the world bowing at their royal feet. The Tigress is prepared to reward those who hold her in this high esteem generously. Both of these extraordinary women are great humanitarians who have devoted their lives to the service of others. For relieving the sufferings of those along her path, and for endeavoring to make this world a better place, the noble Tigress wins the "good karma of the millennium" award.

The Tiger Man

Whether disassembling the undercarriage of a car to rescue a trapped kitten or dodging bullets as an implanted war reporter, Ray is the personification of energy and nobility. He is blessed with a natural advantage over others and possesses an authoritarian presence. No doubt here who is in charge. Ray actively searches for new revolts and adventures. Lulls, relaxation, and inactivity make him squirm and the tempo of his life is fast, fearless, and exhausting.

Not surprisingly, Ray's favorite sport and passion is auto racing. This natural for Nascar pictures himself in the driver's seat as he follows the action. Unfortunately, he has accumulated an impressive number of speeding tickets of his own contending for urban pole position. Ardent for the absolute, Ray challenges the status quo and authority in general. Rebellious and impulsive, he resists controls at every turn.

Ray is the first one to jump in to break up a dog fight or rescue a terrified child caught in the middle of a wartime firefight. It is important for him to take time to reload his energy munitions and find wholesome coping mechanisms. Sports are an excellent outlet for him, but from early childhood this adventurous young man has suffered from twisted joints, fractures, and scars. While "action without hesitation" is a wonderful quality when working in emergency situations, the result on Ray has been numerous casualties. His is a soul that is invaluable in resolving difficult problems and situations. His get-up-and-go attitude makes him a bold innovator in all fields. As a friend, his loyalty is unsurpassed and he fiercely protects those he calls his own.

Damien is a large and imposing man. His muscular stature and vitality are readily apparent and it is easy to see why this "Samson" of the Zodiac is enticingly attractive to women.

As does Ray, Damien needs large and difficult projects to conquer. He knows how to put time limits on his dreams and transform them into attainable goals. Optimistic and goal-oriented, the walls of his office are covered with honors and awards of appreciation.

However, conquest, not reward, is the name of Damien's game. Never afraid to challenge the powers that be, he has successfully battled the powerful and the influential, exposing scandals and reversing injustices.

Damien enjoys being out in the midst of nature, exploring untried paths. Adventuresome and intent on living life on the edge, Damien doesn't merely hike, fish and camp—he works with the Nation Forest

Service to help capture sick or injured wild animals. He has wrestled crocodiles, subdued large cats, and assisted in many "rescues" of exotic creatures for medical care and sanctuary. Consequently, as his Tiger brother Ray, Damien bears the marks and scars of his heroism. His destiny ebbs and flows with extremes, resembling gentle waves alternating with the violent swells of a tsunami.

Despite being obstinate, Damien is well liked and respected for his candor and sincerity. "What you see is what you get" with this passionate soul who seldom deliberates too long or misses opportunities. Stealthily and confidently he strides ahead with unlimited enthusiasm virtually devoid of egoism or small-mindedness. However, his generosity and sympathy for those less fortunate doesn't extend to those who are intentionally spineless or wishy-washy. Haste and pride remain his greatest foes.

Damien is a karmic risk-taker who is wired for leadership. He has a taste for innovation and untried approaches, but is not always successful. Financially, Damien has suffered his share of ups and downs, and has changed professions dozens of times.

Both Ray and Damien, despite their contrasted backgrounds, share an honest and forthright character. An old-fashioned sense of chivalry and decency is at the core of their psychology. No mountain is too tall or ocean too wide for the heroic Tiger man to surmount. Ray sums it up nicely when he says, "I like to practice what I preach."

The Rabbit/Cat

The Detached Rabbit (Mao)— the "Artful Dodger"

January 29, 1903 to February 15, 1904: Water Rabbit
February 14, 1915 to February 2, 1916: Wood Rabbit
February 2, 1927 to January 22, 1928: Fire Rabbit
February 19, 1939 to February 7, 1940: Earth Rabbit
February 6, 1951 to January 26, 1952: Metal Rabbit
January 25, 1963 to February 12, 1964: Water Rabbit
February 11, 1975 to January 30, 1976: Wood Rabbit
January 29, 1987 to February 16, 1988: Fire Rabbit
February 16, 1999 to February 4, 2000: Earth Rabbit
February 3, 2011 to January 22, 2012: Metal Rabbit

Polarity: yin (negative)
Sign order: fourth
Alternate name: Cat
Symbolism: abundant
  reproduction
Lucky color: aqua
Fragrance: patchouli/musk

Flavor: sweet and sour
Food/beverage: rice, fish,
  white wine
Flowers: daffodil, hyacinth
Gem: aquamarine
Feng shui direction: east
Lucky Number: four

The fourth position in the Chinese Zodiac, the Rabbit, is one of good judgment and refined creativity. Those souls born into Rabbit years learn the lesson of "detachment"—the ability to separate and to alternate between sociability and retreat. The Rabbit soul has a need for comfort and privacy, and requires freedom from disturbance and disorder.

The Rabbit is wild by nature, difficult to domesticate, and resists being pinned down. In Chinese folklore it is said that the Rabbit will always have three exits to its burrow, allowing escape at will. This sensitive sign is fine-tuned to feelings and auditory sounds, and has its paw on the pulse of life. This offers the Rabbit exceptional insight into creative and detailed work. A Rabbit prefers to keep their own counsel, listen only to their inner intuition, and rarely acts on unsolicited advice.

Rabbits side-step disruption artfully due to their even tempers and calm nature. When a Rabbit needs personal space they may vanish, reappearing when rested and when personal composure has been restored. Rabbits have a remarkable ability to heal from psychological as well as physical wounds.

Both cautious and conservative, aloof yet charming, the Rabbit is a kind and helpful friend. The virtuous Rabbit possesses a highly developed sense of justice and fairness. This makes them much sought after for their mediation skills and diplomacy. The favorable time of day for the Rabbit is between 5 a.m. and 7 a.m., just as the sun is rising and when the yin power peaks. These are the rejuvenation hours of refuge and sanctuary.

Essential Temperament

Cautious Rabbits contend with difficulties in life by limiting contact with chaos and confusion. Negative external influences can disrupt their creativity, especially the artists, musicians, and other right-brain creators. Peace at all costs is essential for their creative flow.

Rabbits are virtuous companions, discreet and exceedingly gifted in persuasion. In an emergency they can be counted on to lend assistance, and they are compassionate and devoted friends. Rabbits are squeamish where bloodshed is concerned, but shine in the role of understanding counselor. They dissect situations and analyze options.

Rabbits tend to worry about their health more than actually necessary. While not hypochondriacs, Rabbits take even small health matters quite seriously and tend to them without delay. Rabbit natives may be susceptible to stomach, digestive, and intestinal difficulties, are also vulnerable to environmental insults such as pollution and excessive noise.

Rabbits rarely complain of being lonely. They prefer their own company or the company of a select handful of close friends. Intimate gatherings of select guests are usually preferred to noisy social gatherings. Rabbits are so independent that their only real need is a comfortable, secure home and unlimited personal time.

The Rabbit's gentle and sensitive nature makes them easily troubled by abrupt environmental changes at home or at work. Loud noises, pollutants, brawls, and strong emotional stimuli overwhelm their delicate senses. However, due to their active interest in healthy food and nutritional programs, Rabbits do enjoy long and healthy lives.

The Other Side—the Rabbit's Duality

In contrast to their many admirable attributes, unenlightened Rabbits can be aloof, secretive, and easily offended. Rabbits run from being forced to choose sides or make difficult choices. As one of the most sexual of the signs, disturbed Rabbits are capable of being downright libertine in their debauchery and perversions. Leisure activities are enjoyed as long as they don't feel the responsibility for either the planning or the outcome. Rabbits hate to take the blame for plans gone awry (or anything for that matter). Pedantic Rabbits excel at "passing the buck" to others, and the more manipulative Rabbits make for infuriating bureaucrats. Self-centered and suspicious behavior represents the Rabbit's energy being directed in its most unproductive form. It is for this reason that some Rabbits have difficulty forming interpersonal relationships of long duration. Expressed in its darkest form, this energy becomes cowardice, narcissism, self-absorption, materialism, and commitment-phobia. The choice lies completely with the individual. Taken to the extreme, narcissistic, histrionic, and paranoid personality disorders may develop.

Gifts and Capabilities

Reserved Rabbits are individuals of high moral standing. Their excellent taste and gracious manners are distinct, and Rabbit souls are defined by sophistication and refinement. They are also not easily provoked. They enjoy a calm nature as placid pacifists. The Rabbit is more sentimental than truly sensitive, and therefore more disturbed by personal stresses and upheaval than by foreign wars or world hardships.

According to legend, the Rabbit will have the most peaceful existence when they avoid an emotional overload and a dramatic turn of events. Wars, revolutions, and unpleasant emotional outbursts are intolerable to them. Rabbits were not designed for adversity or high-drama situations. Anything that threatens their quiet life becomes unbearable, and if they do not remove themselves from these situations, their mental health can seriously suffer.

Once rejuvenated, the Rabbit emerges ready to play. This private soul then becomes surprisingly social and entertaining. The more reserved Rabbits stick to writing or the fine arts and prefer to remain a "behind the scenes" influence. The more outgoing of this sign are performers, musicians, high-finance brokers, and diplomats of state. Rabbits possess a wonderful sense of humor and make entertaining conversationalists and colorful storytellers.

Although essentially introverted, Rabbits have a strong need to be liked and accepted. Rabbits are touchy on the inside yet remain calm on the outside. They effectively control outward displays of emotion and few will be privy to their inner feelings.

The Child

The Rabbit as a baby and young child is a joy to their parents. Even the most critical parent describes a Rabbit child as "a good kid." Rabbit children need little discipline and seem to police themselves. They are, however, hypersensitive to direct criticism and dislike any kind of family fighting or upset. They run from confrontations and will always be the peacemakers of the group. This child may be gifted in one of the fine arts such as music, art, voice, or dance, and should be provided exposure to and cultivation of these talents.

Rabbit children use their charming sense of humor to smooth over tense situations. Always the diplomat, this child strives to quell conflicts and must maintain a healthy distance from the tragic and depressing in life. This is an aesthetic and auditory child, soothed by pleasing sounds, beautiful music, and interesting personal gossip. Rabbit youngsters may seem aloof at times and have a strong need for personal space.

Home and Hearth

Rabbits love their families, but they are not known to be particularly family-oriented. Rabbit parents, being essentially private, often seem more like detached observers rather than active participants in their children's lives. They are sensitive and capable of being deeply wounded, and must keep a healthy distance from disruptive influences in their life. Unfortunately, this can manifest as an inability to cope with noisy offspring, crying babies, and the topsy-turvy existence that constitutes raising children.

A rested and relaxed Rabbit parent is humorous and entertaining. A jostled Rabbit is brittle, moody, and will feel the need to flee the

source of distress. Rabbits need quite a bit of time to tinker, to rumi-
nate, and to read. They also hunger for sufficient finances to deco-
rate, beautify, and make comfortable their private nooks.

The most favorable time of year for the Rabbit is mid-April to mid-
May, when plants and flowers are in full bloom and life is renewed with
reproduction and sexuality. Favorite places are nighttime silent paths
close to their cozy home, or amongst the forest wilderness.

Auspicious Careers

Whether as a philosopher, a diplomat, an administrator, a politician, or a priest, Rabbits function well in almost any role except that
of frontline fighter. In business, as in friendship, the Rabbit gets along
with almost everyone. They have a knack for adapting themselves to
circumstances. Gifted in the arts, many Rabbits excel in music, performing, dance, voice, and other forms of the fine arts. In diplomatic
situations, where tact and utmost discretion is critical, the Rabbit will
shine. Good career choices for the Rabbit include diplomat or am-
bassador, artist (any medium), publicist, public relations specialist,
performer, commercial or financial advisor, musician/composer, attorney, magistrate, judge, stockbroker, high-fashion model, beauti-
cian, and designer or interior decorator.

The Famous and the Infamous

Some notable Rabbits include: Nicolas Cage, Brad Pitt, Elisabeth Shue,
Drew Barrymore, John Cleese, Quentin Tarantino, Jet Li, Kate Winslet,
Helen Hunt, Tori Amos, Ming-Na Wen, Johnny Depp, James Galway,
Bob Hope, John Hurt, Michael Keaton, Brigitte Nielsen, Tatum O'Neal,
Jane Seymour, Frank Sinatra, Martin Luther, Confucius, Albert Einstein,
Queen Victoria, Orson Wells, Arturo Toscanini, Arthur Miller, Longfellow,
Walt Whitman, Wilbur Wright, Andy Warhol, Henry James, George C.
Scott, Judy Collins, Francis Ford Coppola, Anjelica Huston, and Sting.

Summary

Thoughtful Rabbit, thank you for being such a good friend! When we need hot soup or a sympathetic ear, you are always there. This world can seem overwhelming to your delicate sense of balance. Know that you are stronger than you think you are. Push past the fear, which can immobilize you. Your sense of virtue can lead you down the road of perfectionism, which may derail the course of friendships and love. Flowers may bloom again, but remember that a person never has the chance to be young again. Cherish your time and don't let opportunities pass you by. Go ahead and take that plunge!

You are the stranger
I have known forever.
Your touch
Numbs yesterday's pain.
How did you know
I thirst for something gentle
In a world that puts thorns
Even on roses?

The Rabbit Woman

Cara is a delicate and quiet beauty. Stylishly dressed, her conservative business suit sports a feminine lace camisole peeking from the lapel. Her beautiful eyes and flawless skin are but two of her exquisite features. Despite her awesome femininity, this lady is pragmatic and makes use of reason. Her artistic perceptions and sense of discretion are amazing, as is her advice, which is time-tested and practical.

In spite of her competence, Cara is perfectly content in a creative role and prefers to leave the mundane work of running the business to her partner. Observant, charming, and socially at ease, her talent for interior decorating is highly sought after. Refinement, creativity, and sensitivity are her most invaluable qualities.

Cara is also very smart at handling money (both her own and other peoples'). Happiest when she is not personally responsible for an outcome, Cara has the ability to analyze any dilemma, however complex, down to the finest detail.

However, despite her outward competence and composure, Cara is plagued by enough personal doubts to be intimidated by life at times. Similar to her Dog sisters, Cara worries about many things, and is especially anxious about her own health. She maintains a strict diet and vitamin regimen in hopes of preventing any possible malady. When her children stub a toe or have a nosebleed, Cara calls in the cavalry. This is a lady who is very squeamish and prefers to leave the doctoring to others.

Cara was most reluctant to give her heart away and it took her husband four years to persuade her to marry him. Being more sensitive than truly passionate, Cara never allows her heart to rule over her cautious and skeptical mind. A long courtship was necessary for Cara to feel comfortable with her decision to make a permanent commitment. Cara's husband has never sought to dominate her, which is one of the main reasons they enjoy a harmonious marriage. He knows she needs plenty of privacy, quietude, and time for contemplation. She would be happier alone than with a man who is insensitive, loud, or rude. In exchange for his kindness, Cara is a sweet, attentive, and supportive wife, loyal to her husband's interests and fully capable of contributing to his vocational success. She is an entertaining and aware companion who is also competent to counsel.

Cara is a wonderful cook and hostess. Her guests enjoy good food, good wine, and good conversation. Socially, she is the consummate "muse," inspiring creativity and freedom of thought. Emotional, yet controlled, she is a compassionate friend and is deeply concerned with the welfare of others.

Cara had difficulty becoming pregnant due to gynecological problems stemming from a hormonal imbalance. This same etiology has been responsible for other various "female" disorders, such as ovarian cysts and irregular menstrual periods. Prevention is the best policy and the Chinese herb Dong Quai has been helpful in lessening her discomforts and regulating her reproductive system. As do her Rabbit brothers, Cara also has an extremely touchy nervous system, and she must keep a healthy distance from overwhelming emotional drama and catastrophes.

Fellow Rabbit Marie is considerate and kind. Her home has the cozy feel of a settled and quiet lifestyle. Marie lives happily there with her boyfriend of 18 years and sees no reason to "jeopardize" the relationship with marriage. She has chosen not to have her own children, but is an involved and loving aunt to her two nieces. The girls look forward to spending time with Marie, whether searching out the latest fashions, or just spending a quiet day by the pool. Both girls know that they can tell Marie anything and always come to her first for advice.

Both Cara and Marie are aesthetic perfectionists; blessed and cursed with hypersensitive consciences. Each must pace themselves and regulate their energies. Each of these modest and unobtrusive women requires a significant amount of privacy and indulgence for emotional happiness.

The Rabbit Man

Joey's psychological world is a private one. Others identify him by his friendly, jovial personality, strewn with humorous tidbits and amusing antidotes. He is a welcome guest at any party or social function and Joey thrives in these social situations where he is more than glad to sing, play the flute, and entertain his comrades. Joey is a one-man show. Physically, he is of short stature, and his soft-spoken and cautious mannerisms may go unnoticed. He prefers to keep a low profile until he chooses to focus the spotlight in his direction.

Joey possesses a natural gift for music, dancing, and the fine arts. His eye is keen for beauty and his ear fine-tuned to melodies from within. Silence and the midnight hour are his bedfellows. Sadly, his artistic temperament and solitary lifestyle have derailed the course of love in his life and Joey, at age 50, has never been married. He prefers the company of his chosen "friends" over blood ties, as they don't assign responsibility to him for their lives or happiness. Joey openly admits he's not a "family man."

Joey is also not a "frontline" fighter, and is the first person to exit from a tense situation or peril. While his Tiger brothers are carrying people out of a burning building, this much more fragile man is long gone down the street. While cowardly is too strong a word, Rabbit males do instinctually escape anything and everything that could potentially trigger their inner tensions, upset their emotional balance, or cause them physical injury.

Being fearful and fretful about his health, Joey is well versed on any new health craze. He sports a well-stocked cabinet of pharmaceuticals, herbal remedies, and various touted tonics. His digestive system can be touchy, and he is very fussy about the type and quality of the food that he eats. However, as middle age has come upon him, obesity, from an increasingly sedentary lifestyle, is his greatest concern.

Joey's "Yin" soul is by and large introverted, and he jealously protects his secluded lifestyle. His amplified sensitivity and brittle emotional balance require him to maintain his distance from potential disruption or intrusion. He is "hard to read," and even those who consider themselves close to him are rarely privy to his inner thoughts and intentions. When involved in a creative project, he is so exclusively focused that the world around him ceases to exist.

After years of missed opportunities in love, Joey has become emotionally numb, disillusioned, and even somewhat cynical. His search for perfection and virtue has been long and arduous. His quest for the "perfect" woman has been fruitless, as no such female exists. She would have to be a combination of *all* women really, in a word—an angel. This is a soul who is suspicious of romance and distrusts sentiments—even his own. Joey is contemptuous of the institution of marriage and by choice remains a confirmed bachelor. He continues to pursue his dreams of musical fame and fortune; he is in a perpetual state of pubescence, living in a fringe world of cabarets and nightclubs.

George, while sharing the same dislike for chaos and confusion as Joey, has chosen a much different path for his life. George uses his profound diplomacy skills as a clinical psychologist. Always the peacemaker, he specializes in family counseling and working with troubled adolescents. His mature, sensitive nature, combined with an understanding and remembrance of his own youth, make him an invaluable family mediator.

Possessing a superbly analytical mind, George is capable of mastering any subject and has an impressive personal library. He is well read on many subjects and can discuss them intelligently, even with experts in the field.

Like Joey, George prefers solitude or the company of a few valued friends to crowded or formal affairs. He balks at gallivanting around the country; he usually stays behind to catch up on his reading while his wife is traveling. George waited until his late 30s to marry and now has a daughter who is the apple of his eye. He is a gentle and dedicated father who is never too busy to lend an understanding ear.

While far from sanctimonious, George believes in self-improvement and faithfully practices the martial arts. Interested in cultivating both mind and body, he strives to attain excellence in everything he does. A fair and impartial judge of human nature, George has a deep sense of morality and justice. He is honest, tactful, and an excellent friend.

"Time is on my side" is a favorite saying of both Joey and George, and both men are supremely patient. Both souls also hold strong and deep convictions. Joey, however, is an island unto himself, while George immerses himself in assistance to others. Joey has composed a life opera of narcissism and seclusion, while George has created a destiny of fellowship and connection.

Chapter 7

The Dragon

The Unpredictable Dragon (Chen)— the "Theatrical Visionary

February 16, 1904 to February 3, 1905: Wood Dragon
February 3, 1916 to January 22, 1917: Fire Dragon
January 23, 1928 to February 9, 1929: Earth Dragon
February 8, 1940 to January 26, 1941: Metal Dragon
January 27, 1952 to February 13, 1953: Water Dragon
February 13, 1964 to February 1, 1965: Wood Dragon
January 31, 1976 to February 17, 1977: Fire Dragon
February 17, 1988 to February 5, 1989: Earth Dragon
February 5, 2000 to January 23, 2001: Metal Dragon
January 23, 2012 to February 9, 2013: Water Dragon

Polarity: yang (positive)
Sign order: fifth
Symbolism: transformation
Lucky color: crimson red
Fragrance: tea rose
Flavor: pungent, sharp

Food/beverage: poultry, juices
Flower: sweet pea
Gem: diamond
Feng shui direction: east-southeast
Lucky number: two

The fifth position in the Chinese Zodiac, the Dragon, is one of mystery, vitality, and the universe itself. Those souls born into Dragon years learn the lesson of "unpredictability"—others can only guess which hat the Dragon chooses to wear on any given day.

Shrewd and enthusiastic, the Dragon is the sign with the greatest power and the most powerful influence. Unlike the other animals of the Chinese Zodiac, the Dragon is a mythical creature, and the sign of good luck and vital health. Unlike the frightening Dragon of Western mythology, Chinese Dragons are benevolent creatures that live in the heavens and amongst the wind, mist, rain, thunder, and lightning. A Dragon needs oxygen, freedom, and open space to thrive. Contact with the outdoors and nature is most important for physical and emotional health.

Tenacious and captivating, Dragons like to stay in motion, stay preoccupied, and stay busy. The Dragon symbolizes life and growth, as reflected in their generous and scrupulous nature. Full of Utopian ideas and bursts of energy, Dragons have the power to influence, to lead, and to impress.

Dragons have a keen intuition and see life as a rainbow of possibilities. Dragons neither require, nor do they seek out, constant reassurance. Confident, ambitious, and brave, a Dragon will work, sometimes from morning until night, in an effort to keep things running properly, and they are capable of taking aggressive action if necessary. This soul will defy obstacle after obstacle in an effort to climb their way to the top of their field.

The most harmonious time of day for Dragons is between 7 a.m. and 9 a.m., when the yang force, still unsteady but awesomely powerful, rises and makes transformations. For those born into Dragon years, each new day is a new page in the diary, a new step toward an idea or project, and they greet life at the peak of their strength in the morning hours.

Essential Temperament

No matter what Dragons choose to do with their lives, they will shine; it is their nature to excel. The Dragon just cannot help but win. Free spirits make up the majority of those born in Dragon years, and Dragons possess greater intuition than other signs. According to Chinese tradition, the weather conditions at the time of a Dragon's birth have a great deal of influence on the course of their lives. It is thought that a Dragon born during a storm will lead a tempestuous and hazardous life, possibly involving dangerous or spectacular experiences. One born on a day when the sea (the Dragons ancestral home) and the heavens are calm will have a protected existence and a more peaceful nature.

Seldom do Dragons enjoy sitting behind a desk. They detest tedious routine, especially being stuck in a web of boring duties and obligations. While Dragon souls hate to take orders, they enjoy giving them, making this the sign of natural leaders.

When Dragon natives feel compelled to speak their mind, watch out. Nothing will silence them. This outspoken nature stems from much youthful yang energy influencing this sign. It is considered a futile effort to fight a Dragon. They feel they have been granted authority by divine right. A wounded Dragon never forgets an insult. Dragons make the most formidable enemies anyone could imagine. Their ruthlessness is matched only by the power of their influence. The best thing to do if in conflict with those born into Dragon years is to avoid them until you can make sincere amends.

The Dragon enjoys being called upon to help when things go wrong. The Dragon will succeed where others have failed both because the word *impossible* is not in their vocabulary, and because they simply must champion extreme situations. However, this soul can be overpowering, and being unable to give less than their best is exhausting but necessary for them. The best role for a Dragon is as a visionary or prophet and dreamer of Utopian imagery. The worst role is that of diplomat, as Dragons lack tactfulness.

The sky is a favorite place for those born into Dragon years. Favorite leisure activities for Dragons include philosophy, arcane sciences, science fiction, the cosmos, exploration of the universe, or anything that takes them far away from the Earth. This "otherworldly" nature is most characteristic of the sign.

The Other Side—the Dragon's Duality

In contrast to their many admirable attributes, unenlightened Dragons can be short-tempered, demanding, and brutally candid. Being a soul of extremes, the Dragon's energy channeled negatively can cause great destruction. An egotistic Dragon can be so overbearing one would think they rule by divine right. Another unflattering characteristic of shallow Dragons is infidelity. Dragons are capable of maintaining a completely separate life from their primary relationship, sometimes for years. They seem perfectly capable of keeping their dual life discreet and undetected from an unsuspecting partner.

Egotistic and judgmental behavior represents the Dragon's energy being directed in its most unproductive form. Dragons can feel a certain sense of entitlement to say whatever is on their mind, many times with jaw-dropping results. Expressed in its darkest form, this energy becomes easy infatuation, harshness, stubbornness, belligerence, infidelity, impetuousness, and malcontent. The choice lies entirely with the individual. Taken to extreme, borderline personality disorders may develop, and there is a propensity for Dragons to suffer from bipolar disorders.

Gifts and Capabilities

A Dragon is both lucky and gifted, and they will always find people to believe in them. However, Dragons are sometimes accused of being reckless, getting involved too quickly, and not thinking about future monthly payments. They often fail to see the dishonesty in others;

therefore, they get cheated or swindled on occasion. When Dragons have money they tend to spend it quickly. A Dragon's bank account will often be well filled, but the cash may be withdrawn as quickly as it is deposited. It is a good idea for a Dragon to have the Ox, with their financial foresight, or the scrupulous and honest Pig as a business associate.

Dragons are claustrophobic and need space. Dragons can also become depressed if forced to live in the same mundane surroundings for a long time. If they cannot travel, they certainly need exotic furniture and a change of style often. A mural of a desert island on the living-room wall or a splash of some bright paint on the walls can do wonders for their peace of mind at home. The perfect abode for this magnificent creature is a fortified castle perched on a rocky ravine, and overgrown with lush grottoes. The Dragon's love of travel could draw them to these exotic places at some time in their life.

In general, Dragons are physically healthier than most people, but they need to pay attention to dangers relating to stress and the internal struggle of a bipolar temper. Dragon people desire many friends and have an overwhelming need to be loved in order to thrive. Intense and possessive in romance, they are at the same time somewhat doubtful and reserved. Dragon love affairs are magnificently dramatic. They possess plenty of youthful yang energy to keep love alive during the good times, as well as during the occasional thunderstorms.

Those born into Dragon years expect people to look upon them with admiration and to always take their advice. They will stimulate your spirit of competition and taste for conquest. The principal qualities of the Dragon are activity, energy, and, above all, fortune and good luck. A restrained Dragon can be demanding, impatient, and intolerant. A Dragon who becomes trapped in life with little room to maneuver will suffer and become disillusioned, roaring to be free from the confinement. The infamous temper of this powerful soul can explode in fury when not met with respect. When the thunder and lightning has ended, the rainbow comes; the Dragon returns once again to their witty, open, and honorable presence.

The Child

"Mommy, why is that lady so fat?" Many a red-faced parent has learned firsthand how outspoken Dragon children are. Colicky and rather demanding from the day they are born, in the pediatric nursery, Dragon babies will be the first to get fed by virtue of volume. They will be noticed. Dragons are willful and powerful children. This little "showman" may lack tact at times, but is always reached by sentimentality.

The Dragon child feels that certain tasks are beneath them. These kids may balk at taking out the trash, cleaning their rooms, and other boring or mundane tasks.

Dragon babies and children are the healthiest and most long-lived of the Zodiac and rarely get sick. They exude vitality. This will not be a clingy or whining child, as even from childhood the Dragon is fiercely independent and self-assured. Many physicians and stage actors were born into Dragon years.

Home and Hearth

Regarding family affairs, Dragon parents are proud and have no patience for challenges of authority from their children. They are giving of themselves in emotional circumstances, and make compassionate yet stern parents. Dragon parents are also unequaled in their ability to encourage independence in their children. However, Dragon mothers do not like being only relegated to domestic life, and strive to combine family responsibilities with professional aspirations.

The most favorable time of year for the Dragon is mid-May to mid-June, the most vibrant and prosperous months of the year, when flowers are at peak bloom and foliage is lush and green.

Auspicious Careers

As a career choice, the Dragon makes an excellent actor, artist, trial lawyer, gangster, priest, prophet, doctor, or business owner. Being a doer, the Dragon does best in independent professions. They are known to lead demonstrations, crusades, write letters to newspapers, and collect a million signatures on a petition. When it comes to their work, Dragons are determined and committed, but impatient with those who do not share their calling. In business, the Dragon is encouraged to seek partners who match their strength, rather than those less forceful. Tigers and Monkeys can handle well the Dragon's boldness, and they will work by their side without fear of being engulfed or overshadowed.

The Famous and the Infamous

Some well-known Dragons include: Robin Williams, Roseanne Barr, Deng Xiaoping, Courtney Cox, Keanu Reeves, Sandra Bullock, Alicia Silverstone, Dan Aykroyd, Julia Ormond, Patrick Stewart, Calista Flockhart, Sarah Bernhardt, Salvador Dali, Sigmund Freud, Joan of Arc, Bing Crosby, Neil Diamond, Placido Domingo, Bo Diddley, Tom Jones, John Lennon, Ringo Starr, Raquel Welch, Pearl Buck, Lewis Carroll, Lady Godiva, J. Paul Getty, Marlene Dietrich, Faye Dunaway, Joan Baez, Frank Zappa, Mae West, Joseph Campbell, Shirley Temple Black, and Dr. Ruth Westheimer.

Summary

Powerful Dragon, you inspire us all with your Utopian dreams and spectacular accomplishments. Thank you for riding up on your white horse when disaster strikes. This world is indeed your stage and you have our attention, but must you speak so freely? Remember, it is not necessary to say everything that crosses your mind. A weak person is liable to be bullied; a tamed horse is often ridden. You feel that weakness is a disadvantage and that if you are not tough, you will be bullied. Be aware that there are those whose skin is much thinner than yours and don't understand your outspoken ways. Endear yourself to others by showing them that delightfully sentimental heart of yours!

Houselights dim,
The curtain of night rises as
Orion enters
Center stage.

The Dragon Woman

All eyes are fixed on Deborah when she enters a room. Strikingly beautiful and radiating self-confidence, she is fully aware of her effect on those around her. Her stunning auburn hair cascades down her back and she carries herself with an air of distinction and dignity.

Blessed with good health and vital life Qi, Deborah is resilient, busy, and excitable. Short-tempered and impatient, she wisely chooses to channel her intense energy through t'ai chi and qi gong. Philosophy and physical movement help her to be less aggressive, more in control of her emotions, and better able to relax her kaleidoscopic mind.

She will admit to being rather extravagant with money, and although she thoroughly enjoys luxuries and splendor, she is also very generous. Deborah always brings a gift of some kind when she comes to visit, and holidays with her are absolutely lavish.

Deborah has begun to turn her pastime of studying astrology into a small consulting practice. But never confining herself to the mundane, she is also in the process of completing the requirements for professional astrological certification. She possesses a superior intellect combined with an otherworldly intuition. If her Tiger sisters are the "empresses" of the Zodiac, Dragoness Deborah is indisputably the "high priestess."

Deborah's fair and visionary nature allows her to see both sides of a controversy. Her frankness and balanced outlook invites others to trust her. She is not interested in a person's financial status, nor would she ever befriend someone (or marry) because of their money. Her idealism and ability to visualize the future, combined with practical good sense, make her a natural leader. Deborah's ability to adapt to new situations and places, and her aptitude for foreign languages, have been invaluable during her travels. Whether it is the aboriginal tribes of New Guinea, or the Marsh Arabs of Iraq, Deborah has studied their culture and bubbles over with little-known facts.

Opal is the undisputed "matriarch" of her family. When disaster strikes, this is the woman you will want to call. Capable and efficient, she will do everything in her power to remedy the situation. Born the oldest child of migrant farmworkers, Opal assumed a position of authority and responsibility early in life. Hardship is no stranger to her and life's difficulties only serve to bring out her finer qualities. Her self-confidence is immense and no challenge is too great for her to tackle.

Dramatic and enthusiastic by nature, Opal, like her Dragon brothers, enjoys being the center of attention. She resents being relegated to second in command and will bluntly tell you so! Tact and discretion are not exactly her strong points. Despite her amazing energy at age 70, she longs to retire and live the easy life. She would love nothing more than to whisk herself away to unhurriedly explore foreign countries and cultures. But alas, too many people look to her for care and guidance. She is their rock and she knows this.

Opal, married to her Tiger husband for over 50 years, was blessed with a wide range of capabilities. She worked side by side as a complete equal with her husband as they successfully built and ran their own business and raised four children. This loyal and devoted soul has cheered on countless football games and spilled tears of joy at her daughter's numerous operatic recitals. One might say that her daughter has a little of her Dragon mothers' "love of the spotlight" in her.

Both Deborah and Opal are souls who need to be praised and admired. No matter what fate presents to them, the Dragoness will hold fast to her independence, forever destined to be honored and adored.

The Dragon Man

Daniel's enthusiasm and intensity are not for the faint of heart. His soul and presence exude confidence and a powerful life force. Admiration and respect are the fuels that run his life-engine. His image is of supreme importance to him, and he is completely at home occupying center stage. Daniel's roguish good looks and theatrical penchant have brought him great success in motion pictures and on stage. This is not a gentleman who takes a backseat to anyone or anything, and he is the consummate "leading man."

A natural showman from day one, Daniel knows the way to excite others to action. Daniel's oratory skills are keen, and he speaks with authority, exuberance, candor, and an outstanding wit. Opinionated and a master at combining charm and influence, Daniel has an extraordinary ability to generate enthusiasm. Those who work with him have the utmost respect for his authority. This prince of the podium is absolutely irresistible to a crowd. Daniel is dynamic, scrupulous, and above all—lucky.

Supremely self-confident, Daniel has a high opinion of those who have a high opinion of him, so to speak. He boisterously mocks those who call him an egotist, sloughing off their comments as empty babble. Zealous in life and in love, his ambitious plans are designed for success. This "pioneer" of the Eastern Zodiac specializes in demolishing the old and rebuilding the new. He tears down outmoded structures and obsolete systems, whether physical or ideological.

Scott, in similar fashion, is not acquainted with the terms subservience or self-effacement. Self-sufficiency and pride are the languages he speaks. Akin to his Dragon brothers, Scott actively strives to be where the spotlight shines. However, he has not met with Daniel's same success. Scott struggles with extreme mood-swings and has difficulty staying on an even keel. His marriage has suffered from his bipolar temper, as well as from his marital indiscretions. His feeling of powerlessness brings out the lower vibrations of his soul and causes him to act out in various ways.

Stuck behind a desk editing tedious technical drawings, Scott is nothing less than miserable. He dreams of an exciting career at the jet propulsion laboratory or high atop Mt. Palomar, manning a giant telescope as an esteemed astronomical scientist. Scott feels the need to leave his mark on society or influence the populace in some manner. He views his current position as menial and with no room to dream, and he cannot envision himself trapped there forever. He yearns for important assignments, room to maneuver, and the opportunity to expand his horizons.

However, despite his current situation, Scott has reason to smile. Due to his multiple gifts and interests, it is perfectly normal for this diverse Dragon to dabble in various professions before finding his niche. Scott enjoys good health and will continue to do so as long as he practices moderation, controls his impulsiveness, and adopts a more easygoing attitude toward life.

Both Daniel and Scott quickly tire of tedious repetition and care little about paltry details. Each seeks complete freedom and the opportunity to utilize their inborn inventiveness and imagination. Both men are natural artists and craftsmen. Neither shrink from hard work, nor are they likely to crack under pressure. Although hopelessly unpredictable, one can be assured that both of these colorful and autonomous men will pursue their dreams to a successful conclusion.

Chapter 8

The Snake

The Intuitive Snake (Si)— the "Learned One"

February 4, 1905 to January 24, 1906: Wood Snake
January 23, 1917 to February 10, 1918: Fire Snake
February 10, 1929 to January 29, 1930: Earth Snake
January 27, 1941 to February 14, 1942: Metal Snake
February 14, 1953 to February 2, 1954: Water Snake
February 2, 1965 to January 20, 1966: Wood Snake
February 18, 1977 to February 6, 1978: Fire Snake
February 6, 1989 to January 26, 1990: Earth Snake
January 24, 2001 to February 11, 2002: Metal Snake
February 10, 2013 to January 30, 2014: Water Snake

Polarity: yin (negative)
Sign order: sixth
Alternate name: Serpent
Symbolism: prophecy
Lucky colors: pink, rose
Fragrance: musk, clary sage
Flavor: bitter

Food/beverage: rich sauces, champagne
Flower: lily of the valley
Gem: emerald
Feng shui direction: south-southeast
Lucky number: three

The sixth position in the Chinese Zodiac, the Snake, is one of gathered strength and quiet accumulation of energy. Those souls born into Snake years learn the lesson of "contemplation"—the middle road of temperance and wisdom. Snakes are patient, passive-aggressive, calculating, conservative, and quietly powerful. The Snake's timing is impeccable; they are always ready when the time comes to act. This soul is destined to control from behind the scenes, which allow them to maintain their privacy.

Seductively charming and mysterious, those born into Snake years possess immense wisdom. Outwardly calm and quiet, they are intense and passionate on the inside. The Snake is the sign known for their unmatched physical beauty. Sage advice and flawless skin are the Snake's most awe-inspiring gifts. These souls like an orderly environment and schedule, and require the utmost privacy. Snakes follow through and hate being left "up in the air."

The best time of day for the Snake is between 9 a.m. and 11 a.m., the time when the yang power has fully gathered its strength and the workday begins. Snakes are late risers, not fully awake until the sun has completely risen. They need to absorb the sun's warmth before they are ready for action. Snake people tend to be at their best at this mid-morning time.

Essential Temperament

The Snake senses and feels its way through life. The Snake universally represents spiritual rebirth, elusiveness, and the exploration of life's mysteries. Sophisticated and reserved, the Snake is elegant in speech, dress, and manners. The Snake soul does not indulge in useless small talk or frivolities and are careful about what they say. Some Snakes have a slow or easygoing way of speaking, and they like to ponder concepts, as well as assess and formulate their views and personal theories before speaking.

The evasive and private nature of the Snake is mysterious, and that is the way they prefer it. They conceal their feelings, sharing at their own choosing. The Snake relies on first impressions, feelings, and sympathies rather than the opinions of others. Their finely tuned intuition may make Snakes seem mistrusting of others. However, this is not the case: they are merely selective of whom they choose to allow into their inner world.

The souls born into a Snake year entertain deep thoughts. They are often considered intellectuals and philosophers. They also have the ability to develop their sixth sense to the point of clairvoyance. It is most important for a Snake to find a channel through which they can express their wealth of gifts and ideas. Favorite collectibles for Snakes are works of art, rare books, precious gemstones, or collections of classical music. These items, of course, need to be genuine, as Snakes scorn fakes or reproductions.

The Other Side—the Snake's Duality

In contrast to their many admirable attributes, unenlightened Snakes can be covert, secretive, and extravagant. Snakes insist on quality, and quality can be costly. The flip side to the Snake's extravagance is their stinginess and penny-pinching. They guard their possessions doggedly. This jealous and possessive behavior represents the Snake's energy being directed in its most unproductive form. Expressed in its darkest form, this energy becomes dishonesty, procrastination, stubbornness, vengefulness, lethargy, and odd or eccentric behavior. The choice lies entirely with the individual. Taken to extreme, criminal behavior or schizoid personality disorders may develop.

Gifts and Capabilities

According to the ancient Chinese people, the season in which a Snake is born, as well as atmospheric conditions at birth, will profoundly affect them throughout life. Snakes born into the spring and summer months, during the midday heat, will be the happiest and most prosperous. Those Snakes born at night during a cold winter storm could be vulnerable to danger, as the destiny of the Snake is so sensitive.

The first two phases of the Snake's life should be relatively calm, but during the final phase, their passionate nature will flare up, causing some youthful adventure and a wonderful reverse-aging process.

Snakes are cautious about lending money, and this can cause internal conflict when someone touches their sympathies. Help is most often offered in the form of kindness and assistance rather than cash. However, Snakes are extremely generous with their time, and often counsel, support, or advise the emotionally distraught. Many Snakes are psychiatrists, counselors, or spiritual advisors by profession.

The Snake soul enjoys pleasing others and adores ornamentation. Snakes detest being duped, taken in, or set up as an example. Favorite leisure activities for the Snake include redecorating, rearranging and maintaining treasured possessions, and spending tranquil weekends in the country listening to classical music, reading, or studying the arcane sciences.

The Child

The Snake, as a child, is eager to please and understand their parents, and they love to be treated as an adult. Little Snakes love to be told secrets, and they have an enormous need for affection and tenderness. Little Snakes, however, don't appreciate sharing their parents' affection with their siblings, and they need to feel preferred. This sedate and calm child develops gradually.

Their physical and mental growth does not come in spurts like other children, but rather develops gradually and steadily. Being fair of face and wise beyond their years, these children are sensual, easygoing, and entertain deep thoughts. The passive-aggressive personality of this child prefers to give others enough rope to allow matters to run their course. A predominance of psychiatrists and philosophy professors were born into Snake years.

Home and Hearth

Snakes make understanding parents and are able to put themselves in their children's place. So much so, they struggle with objectivity in their parental role. Snake parents try to understand the perspective of their children. They want to feel their children's experiences, understand their ideas, and appreciate their attitudes. Their children's confidences are safe with their Snake parent, who can keep a secret for life.

The most favorable time of year for the Snake is between mid-June and mid-July, when the hot, bright sun fosters activity and growth among animals, insects, and plants. This is when the Snake is ready to seize opportunities for profit and gain, and ready to test ideas and fulfill private desires.

Favorite places for the snake include lush forest grottoes, or just the opposite: a dry desert environment. They enjoy counting the stars under a crystal-clear sky, or being snug and cozy in their beautifully decorated homes. Everything in the Snake's home is comfortable and designed for pleasuring the senses. Music playing softly; deep, comfortable cushions; perfumed candles; lovely flowers; a well-filled library; and perhaps some fine wines are characteristic of what visitors will see in the home of a Snake. Favorite books include nonfiction, self-help, philosophy, occult sciences, and religion.

Auspicious Careers

The best role for a Snake is as a professor of philosophy, and they are both smooth of tongue and multilingual. Snake women are many times found as high-fashion models, as their physical beauty is legendary. Snake souls also make wonderful teachers, psychiatrists, psychologists, diplomats, ambassadors, astrologers, clairvoyants, and fit well in any profession requiring the skill of divination. The Snake's professional ambition can be defined as "to be able to lead the easy life." Their primary quality of wisdom distances them from work conflicts, rivalries, and other power struggles. Success suits them, and the Snake knows how to use their innate charm to present an idea or outline a program coolly and logically. Snakes will also excel in public relations, or in performing the delicate tasks of a mediator or intermediary. In any kind of work, the Snake will be willful and determined. They believe in physical and mental economy, and organize and calculate their actions so as not to waste effort or energy. The worst role for a Snake is that of an assembly-line worker; it could literally make them ill.

The Famous and the Infamous

Some famous and infamous Snakes include: Pierce Brosnan, Fiona Apple, Charlie Sheen, John Malkovich, Tim Allen, Howard Stern, Mickey Rourke, Mike Oldfield, Linda McCartney, Jaqueline Kennedy Onassis, Aristotle Onassis, Ryan O'Neal, Kim Basinger, Maya Angelou, Oprah Winfrey, Johannes Brahms, Franz Schubert, Abraham Lincoln, Edgar Allan Poe, Indira Gandhi, Mahatma Gandhi, Howard Hughes, Bob Dylan, Rev. Jesse Jackson, Yasser Arafat, John F. Kennedy, J. Paul Getty, Mao Tse-tung, Princess Grace Kelly Rainier, Greta Garbo, Mary Pickford, Dorothy Parker, Andre Previn, Pablo Picasso, Martin Luther King Jr., Queen Astrid, and Franklin D. Roosevelt.

Summary

Sage Snake, we come to you with our problems, and we thank you for lending a patient ear and enlightening us with your wise advice. If "pretty is as pretty does," you are indeed beautiful, both inside and out. Your flawless advice is that of an old soul, weathered by the sands of time. Your motto is "If you drink with a dear friend, a thousand cups are not enough; if you argue with someone, a half of a sentence is too much." You dream of living a comfortable, neighborly life, filled with good times and good friends. Procrastination remains the chink in your armor. Resist the urge to deliberate too long, or missed opportunities may result.

All the edges of myself
Are tightly sealed today.
No one can come in
Am I suffocating,
So tightly closed within myself?

The Snake Woman

When Celeste seductively saunters through a door, those present are convinced they've seen an angel. This personification of femininity has never had a shortage of suitors. Possessing a stunning appearance and equally stunning advice, she is beautiful both inside and out. She loves with intensity and passion, and is highly in tune with her feelings. However, beneath her friendly manner, Celeste is an exceedingly private and discreet woman. She is the consummate counselor of the Zodiac, privy to the secrets and inner turmoil of those around her. Yet despite her close human interactions, she finds it difficult to open up to others or to expose her own inner world.

Acutely conscious of her seductive capacity, Celeste doesn't flaunt or accentuate her feminine attributes. She dresses fashionably, yet tactfully. She is meticulous about her grooming and takes the time to always look her best. Costly clothes, fine jewelry, and exotic perfumes are admittedly her favorite indulgences. However, she needs very little to embellish her already stunning appearance.

As with Celeste, one is immediately struck by Mei Li's outward beauty and poise. This enticing enchantress is curator of a major metropolitan museum. She is also proud of her own collection of classic artworks. Her intelligent and composed persona, combined with impeccable manners, make her a natural hostess. Her soothing and earthy voice has the power to captivate others, and her museum tours are a delight for the senses.

An avid collector and connoisseur of the great art masters, Mei Li is also quite artistically talented. Her sense of beauty, harmony, shape, and color are truly exceptional. She believes that art is one of the highest forms of creativity.

While Mei Li has been amply blessed with an attractive appearance, she has suffered from various health problems, and her health, in general, is delicate. Her renal system has troubled her, and she has suffered with inflammations of the kidney and bladder, as well as ovarian cysts. Increasing her fluid intake has helped significantly, as has the elimination of alcoholic beverages. She also wisely avoids rough sports and rigorous exercise, which could further strain her weak lower back.

As a profoundly feeling soul, Mei Li knows that her physical well-being walks hand in hand with her emotions. She has seen the physical effects of worry and, in contrast, emotional peace. A major life crisis has been known to result in a deluge of physical symptoms. Fastidious and choosy about the food she eats, the cuisine's preparation and appearance are as important to her as the taste of the meal itself. Elegant table settings adorned with her grandmother's hand-tatted linens, her mother's fine china, and a romantic candelabra complete the perfect ambiance.

In contrast to some of her more dispassionate sisters, matters of the heart are of highest importance to Mei Li. She seeks guidance from her heart and follows her intuition—a recipe for perfect timing. This is a woman who detests vulgarity, violence, and disputes. Blessed with the power to rapidly assimilate information, Mei Li is always looking to broaden her education and learn something new. Dialog and the exchange of ideas are very important to her, so long as the subjects have depth and a philosophical nature. Marathon intellectual discussions are the life blood of her temperament.

Never antagonistic, both Mei Li and Celeste belong to the "yin" group of souls—the peacemakers of the Zodiac who seek harmony, acceptance, and approval. Celeste and Mei Li pride themselves on their fair-minded ability to assess the pros and cons of any situation. Tactful and thoughtful, gentle and stable, neither woman has prejudices or biases. Their thoughtful nature, gentle and friendly, always shows respect for others. Born into a year ruled by the vibrations of the Snake, both women have graduated from the life-school of "consideration."

The Snake Man

Robert possesses a "sixth sense." He is one of the nicest human beings one could ever meet. Although masculine and handsome to a fault, there is no doubt that he is in touch with his feminine side. Robert speaks in the language of feelings and is multisensory. He possesses a finely honed intuition and carries the wisdom of the ages within his soul.

This is a man who can completely sweep a woman off of her feet and hold her breathless with his intensity. Seduction is his style, and passion is his partner. Robert lets the ladies come to him, and come they do in droves. He fashions an enticing nest, waiting to surround and to possess the woman of his dreams. Never one to pressure, coerce, or impose himself on others, Robert "enchants" his way through love and through life.

Professionally, Robert is always polite and friendly. But in the courtroom he is as tough as nails. He stubbornly and emotionally argues as a plaintiff attorney for medical malpractice victims. His ability to assess the psychology of a jury is uncanny. His judgment is free from prejudice and is based on his insightful observations. Robert, a thoroughly cultivated Snake, possesses wise answers, mental alertness, and a core stability, all of which serves him well.

Robert is always well dressed and mindful of his appearance. His manners are flawless and his behavior always appropriate for the situation. It is virtually impossible to provoke him into losing his temper. But even then, he retains his composure and is a master of self-control. He is deeply empathetic, and practices moderation and careful deliberation in everything he does.

While generally enjoying good health, Robert's Achilles' heel is his extreme sensitivity to smoke, pollutants, loud noises, and obnoxious individuals. He also has an adverse reaction to extremes in weather and his immediate environment. He thrives in warm, dry climates, and tends to suffer a myriad of aches and pains when faced with the frigid, wet weather that can immobilize him.

Bryce, also born in a year of the Snake, lives a life of intrigue and excitement normally reserved for James Bond movies. This "007" of the Zodiac works as an intelligence operative for the government. Even his nearest and dearest do not know at any given time what secret assignment he is working on. Never immobilized, despite his strong emotions, Bryce is always calm, cool, and collected. Even under the most extraordinary circumstances, his extreme caution prevents him from making hasty decisions or taking imprudent steps. A moralist and philosopher to his core, Bryce's well-thought-out strategies protect those who are placed on the "front lines" of his risky profession.

Since his youth, Bryce has had an aptitude for electronics and audio sound. As an impoverished child of Welsh immigrants, he busily rummaged through the discarded pieces of wire and other treasures left behind the local radio repair shop. This ingenious soul assembled some amazing gadgets, including a rudimentary "wart zapper" made from a large battery and few well-placed wires.

"Doctor" Bryce charged his neighborhood friends two cents to remove each pesky wart. He chuckles today to think that he may have had the first "electro-cauterizing" system up and running 40 years ago. It is not surprising that Bryce specializes in audio surveillance, wire-tapping, and the high-tech aspects of world intelligence.

On his own time, Bryce enjoys theorizing and contemplating the meaning of life. A cozy (and confidential) fireside chat is his idea of a marvelous evening. However,that being second, of course, to his well-known marathon nights of lovemaking. Much has been written regarding the male Snake's sexual prowess—most of it true.

Injurious contact sports such as football and boxing leave him cold, but Bryce is the recipient of quite a few table tennis awards, and moves with speed and agility. Also, in true romantic form, he is an excellent dancer. Other favorite and therapeutic sports include tennis, swimming, and hiking.

Sentimental and reflective, both Bryce and Robert have a judicious sense of fair play. Both men are good listeners, let others express themselves, and are armchair psychiatrists to their friends. Both Robert and Bryce emanate an aura of serenity, and are clearly at peace with themselves. Security conscious and secretly fearful of rejection, both of these circumspect souls scrutinize the world they live in. Each prefers to attract others with honey rather than vinegar, and both men choose the smooth and wide paths through life.

Chapter 9

The Horse

The Decisive Horse (Wu)— the "Great Debater"

January 25, 1906 to February 12, 1907: Fire Horse
February 11, 1918 to January 31, 1919: Earth Horse
January 30, 1930 to February 16, 1931: Metal Horse
February 15, 1942 to February 4, 1943: Water Horse
February 3, 1954 to January 23, 1955: Wood Horse
January 21, 1966 to February 8, 1967: Fire Horse
February 7, 1978 to January 27, 1979: Earth Horse
January 27, 1990 to February 14, 1991: Metal Horse
February 12, 2002 to January 31, 2003: Water Horse
January 31, 2014 to February 18, 2015: Wood Horse

Polarity: yang (positive)
Sign order: seventh
Alternate name: Steed
Symbolism: high noon
Lucky color: sky blue
Fragrance: cedar

Flavor: mild, subtle
Food/beverage: barbecue, merlot
Flower: rose
Gem: moonstone
Feng shui direction: south
Lucky number: eight

The seventh position in the Chinese Zodiac, the Horse, is lively, engaging, and artistic. Those souls born into Horse years learn the lesson of "decisiveness," the ability to choose. This talkative master of dissertation and discourse is independent and outgoing, with a cheerful demeanor and legions of friends. Horses charge into new ventures with the kind of optimism and enthusiasm that make more conservative types cringe. Horses are born to be successful (and succeed more often than not), and are born to be in perpetual motion.

A born leader and eager to help their fellow man, Horses are honorable in intent and inspire others with their optimism and assertive personalities. The athletic Horse leads life's parade. Extroverted, energetic, and defiant against injustice, the Horse gallops valiantly through life, hurdling adversity and obstacles. Their gift of oration equips them to be the consummate "spokespersons" of the Chinese Zodiac. Horses prefer the podium rather than a spectator seat in the audience.

Friendly, intelligent, and independent, noble quests and searches for greener pastures are common traits of those born into Horse years. Always cheerful and gregarious, Horses are usually everyone's favorite party guest. Horses generally look terrific, have plenty of sex appeal, and know how to dress elegantly. They are comfortable in either a tuxedo or blue jeans. Horse souls seek any occasion where there will be plenty of people and social contact. Concerts, theaters, sporting occasions, and parties are activities they especially enjoy.

The most harmonious time of day for Horses is between 11 a.m. and 1 p.m., when the sun is brightest and the yang force is at its peak. Symbolizing strength and vitality, the Chinese word for Horse is "Wu," which literally translates as "high noon."

Essential Temperament

Throughout their lives, Horse souls are instinctively aware of their talents. From childhood on, they prance along life's paths confidently albeit egocentrically. When challenged to obey an order, Horses do so at their leisure. If what is requested seems reasonable, Horses will carry it out with grace and flair. If they have neither time nor respect for an idea, they simply will not do it. They offer neither an excuse nor an explanation. They openly do as they please.

Horses are quite open-minded and generous. They are the most hospitality-conscious sign in the Chinese Zodiac. They thrive on entertaining and often like to cook. When Horses are busy with a project, they are oblivious to time, events, and others around them.

Distraction through activity is the Horse's key to emotional health. Horses need to keep busy. They do home repairs, write plays, audition, play sports, cook, or engage in any project that holds their interest.

A Horse's home is their castle, and they do not take kindly to busybodies who snoop, investigate, or pry into their private lives. They are possessive and good-hearted toward their spouses and children, but must have authority and respect in their household. They work long and hard to provide amply for their families and, in return, they expect utter fidelity and the freedom to be the king or queen of said castle.

The Horse adores voyages, change, and diversity. The Horse often prefers the homes of close friends and hates to be hemmed in or cooped up. A possessive partner can turn their home into a type of domestic "prison." A Horse soul values freedom above all else. They also can be impatient, irritated by wear and tear, and infuriated by teasing that goes beyond certain limits. Horses pay little attention to insincere praise, unrealistic schemes, impossible lovers, and people on power trips.

Horses are perceptive and instinctive, and alert to movements and trends. They are fond of cultural pursuits such as galleries and museums, but sporting events, theaters, and glittery nightspots are their preferred activities. Always the talkative one in the group, the year of the yang Horse spouts many actors, performers, and famous attorneys. A Horse's idea of fun usually involves competition (whether intellectual or physical), and they are both generous winners and gracious losers. Akin to their Dog brothers and sisters, Horses truly comprehend the meaning of fair play.

The Other Side—the Horse's Duality

In contrast to their many admirable attributes, unenlightened Horses can be easily infatuated, hotheaded, and incredibly selfish. The shadow side of the Horse is far from their cheerful and self-assured lighter side. Tactless and ruthless behavior represents the Horse's energy being directed in its most unproductive form. Dysfunctional Horses believe that this world and everything in it belongs to them. Whether it's their house, their car, their school, or their spouse, it's all about them.

Expressed in its darkest form, this energy can become egomaniacal behavior, aggression, rashness, and fanaticism. The choice lies entirely with the individual. Taken to extreme, narcissistic and oppositional/defiant personality disorders may develop.

Gifts and Capabilities

Within the core of this active and charming soul lies a myriad of magical gifts. There is nothing that the Horse cannot do well. The independent Horse is a possessive and sensual lover, making amorous alliances a critical part of the Horse's existence. Any hint of discord or threat of foul play can throw the generally positive Horse into a major spiral of self-doubt. Horse souls are proud and powerful creatures who can fall rapidly in love with another. Silence and lack of communication disturb the Horse, and they need to be emotionally supported, encouraged, and complimented. A little audience approval now and then wouldn't hurt either.

The Horse is an energetic, clever, and physically swift individual. Those born into Horse years are forceful and bold in their actions, moving quickly and confidently through life. They are offensive players with strength and intelligence who advance ambitiously toward new positions in business, investments, and romance. Both male and female Horses are brave and straightforward in communicating their preferences and form strong bonds with other people. Idealistic and humanitarian in character, the Horse is one of the strongest communicators in the Chinese Zodiac and a natural public speaker or politician.

Perseverance is not a Horse's strongest point, so when their interest wanes or the project fails, Horses can fall into despair. However, not one to participate in a "pity party," they will quickly move on to something new. Their disappointment can be soothed by a new interest, a trip, or at the very least, physical exercise. Although attempts to repress anger generally fail, Horses are quick to forgive and forget, and remain eternally optimistic.

The Child

As a baby and young child, this active little tot may well be the family favorite. Little charmers and communicators from the earliest years, they possess the gift of "attractiveness." Horse children are born leaders, and eagerly help out in times of need. Brave and straightforward, the Horse child adores being the center of attention, debating, lecturing, and performing.

Gregarious and extroverted, Horse kids are physical and enjoy all manner of sports and the outdoors. These children love their own home, but prefer to be "on the go," with new places to visit and interesting people to meet. Horses love to go visiting, and neighbors will sometimes joke that they "have an extra child" at times. Horse children, with their sunny personalities, will have legions of friends and move freely and successfully through school life.

Home and Hearth

As a parent, The Horse will always have an active household. A Horse parent is sentimental and does not believe in corporal discipline for their offspring. Instead of punishment, the Horse parent prefers to talk to their children, explaining and reasoning verbally. Eloquence and cajolery find their way into every aspect of the Horse's life.

The most favorable time of year for the Horse is between mid-July and mid-August, when all life is at its peak of growth and has not yet begun the fall/autumn descent toward hibernation. It is at this time when the Horse should make their major life decisions.

Auspicious Careers

The most favorable career choices for the Horse involve close contact with people and plenty of variety. As a sportsperson, athlete, politician, or public speaker, the Horse will be at the top of their game. A person born in a horse year will also do well in politics. The Horse loves to make speeches, has a way with the crowd, and can always sway opinions. In the theater, as both actor and writer, the Horse can find tremendous personal satisfaction and expression. The Horse is an extrovert, needs to be surrounded by people, and enjoys work outdoors. They make good business leaders; they are decisive, and their instincts are sound. Horses speculate wisely, and they know how to turn a bad situation to their advantage. Horses will also be especially successful as artists and craftspeople, adventurers and explorers, designers, lawyers, teachers, professional athletes, skilled technicians, long-distance truck drivers, supervisors, land and geology surveyors, diplomats, travel agents, or public relations specialists.

The Famous and the Infamous

Some famous and infamous Horses include: Kevin Costner, Cindy Crawford, Kirstie Alley, John Travolta, Paul McCartney, Jimi Hendrix, Sam Cooke, Stone Gossard, Janet Jackson, Mike Tyson, Ross Perot, Sean Connery, Clint Eastwood, Joanne Woodward, Barbra Streisand, Harrison Ford, Kathleen Turner, Buffalo Bill Cody, Leonard Bernstein, Frederic Chopin, Vivaldi, Puccini, Degas, Isaac Newton, Louis Pasteur, Rev. Billy Graham, Linda Evans, Aretha Franklin, Ella Fitzgerald, Ingmar Bergman, Neil Armstrong, Rembrandt, Jean Renoir, Samuel Beckett, Davy Crockett, Charlemagne, Khrushchev, Aldous Huxley, e.e. cummings, Ulysses S. Grant, Rutherford B. Hayes, and Theodore Roosevelt.

Summary

Cheerful Horse, the world is your podium and we are all listening intently to your inspiring words. Dissertation and discourse comes so naturally to you that some would say you were "born talking." However, a hefty dose of persistence would be beneficial to your capricious heart. "A long distance tests a Horse's strength, as time reveals a person's true character." As difficult as it may be for you to believe—time *is* on your side. Perseverance is the key to your success. We would never guess by your poise and self-sufficiency that you secretly lack confidence in yourself. There is no need for this, however, as you possess a winning ticket at the racetrack of life. Now spruce up that shiny mane and go inspire your audience!

The path you walk is steep and twisting;
And where it leads is as uncertain as tomorrow.
I have traveled here before you.

Take my hand and we will climb together,
For just ahead there are pastures of understanding.
I have traveled here before you.

The Horse Woman

Tawny's expressive face is always brimming with emotion, which allows others to easily read her mood. She has no "poker face," and is unable to conceal what she is feeling and thinking. Her flamboyant dress and outgoing manner express her extreme independence and rejection of the ordinary. Tawny is a communicator. Her effusive and effervescent speech resembles a fountain of words spilling over with humor, eclectic facts, and political opinions.

Her forthright and frank approach to life exudes self-confidence and well-being. Her athletic figure reveals an active, vigorous lifestyle, and her very presence is electric with energy. This is not a woman who is idle or lazy in any way, shape, or form.

Radiant and sociable, Tawny is a promoter. She publicizes people, places, and events with finesse. Her temperament is mercurial and alternates in accordance with her moods. She is capable of going from optimism to dread or from tranquility to turmoil all in the blink of an eye. Her eyes sparkle, and her resonant voice is distinctive and powerful.

Physically, she must be cautious of her sensitive digestive system, most notably her gallbladder and pancreas. Rich and fatty foods are a no-no. Her strong emotions (especially if repressed) can be the culprit behind many of her various aches and pains, which include allergic hives and other skin breakouts. Due to her active lifestyle, she is susceptible to sprained ankles, twisted knees, and dislocations of the shoulder. She is also at some risk for elbow and wrist fractures.

Tawny is a bold woman, blessed with outstanding strength of purpose, and vigor of the body, mind, and spirit. Once fixed on a goal, she will pursue it with a zealot's conviction. This past year, she carried off the amazing task of organizing and spearheading the largest gathering of psychics and metaphysical practitioners ever assembled in her province. A humanist to her core, Tawny has always had a fascination for the esoteric. From extraterrestrials to auras, astrology to reiki healing, she has explored them all.

Her most precious asset is her unfailing self-confidence. This enthusiastic soul trusts that her abilities and talents are real, and that it is only a matter of time before they are acknowledged. So Tawny "puts herself out there," so to speak, trolling for life's treasures. She is able to generate enthusiasm and support for her projects. Her convincing proposals make others eager to participate. However, Tawny has also been known to take on too much, and has bitten off more than she could chew on more than one occasion. As spectacular as her victories are, these rare failures have been equally monumental. Still, she maintains an attitude of "no guts, no glory."

Always a fighter for her own liberty and the freedom of others, Candice is actively involved in politics. She has helped campaign for many political candidates and has toyed with the idea of running for public office herself. While Candice is much more conservative than Tawny, both women share a need for absolute freedom, and each holds fast to their sometimes unorthodox beliefs. Candice's curiosity, open-minded views, and sincerity make a lasting impression.

Candice chooses friends from diverse walks of life and despises those who look down on those less fortunate. "Have soapbox, will travel" could be her motto, as this is not a woman who remains silent about her causes. She articulately expresses her deeply held convictions with passion. When an issue or subject has hit a nerve with her, she is capable of long-winded pontifications of amazing duration. Candice has a reputation for being argumentative, and insists on having the last word. However, she is easily bruised and her feelings can be hurt if a debate turns hostile or personal.

Candice shares her life with an intelligent and understanding husband who is also quite independent and self-assured. But her love life hasn't always been smooth. Previous relationships have failed due to rivalries and competition between her and her partners. While far from a conventional marriage, Candice enjoys her liberty and has found a life companion. They live together happily with their two cats.

Both of these charming Horse women sincerely enjoy people. Easy to be with, humorous, and vulnerable, both Tawny and Candice are devastated by coldness and rejection. They have very pronounced likes and dislikes, and neither is ever lukewarm or complacent about life. Each soul is wired for human interaction and both remain popular and well-liked.

The Horse Man

Lloyd is a magnificent stallion of a man. Women find him disarmingly handsome and masculine. His thick, coarse hair shines with health and is pulled back over his broad shoulders. Lloyd is a competitor and a sportsman. His robust physique is that of an athlete. He worked his way up through the minor leagues of baseball to his present position as first baseman for a national baseball team. His face is cheerful, and his mannerisms are straightforward and frank; the most notable feature about Lloyd, however, is his rich, baritone voice. His laughter resonates through the dugout, as does his poorly concealed disappointment when the team is down.

Incessantly restless and unable to stand inactivity, the greatest obstacle to his well-being is his excesses. Lloyd loves good food, good wine, and beautiful women. He has been known to push his body's limits beyond good sense. His preference for red meat, rich foods, wine, and expensive cigars is a recipe for future trouble with his delicate liver and digestive system.

Lloyd loves traveling, and being on the road with the team suits him well. He is able to make himself at home just about anywhere, and there is a bit of the "nomad" in him. One can readily picture him wandering about through exotic locations, making legions of new friends on his journeys. Like his Horse-year sisters, constraints on his freedom imprison him. Independence of thought, freedom of speech, and defiance of outmoded traditions define him.

Akin to his Dragon-year brothers, utopian images and future progress is where his attention is focused. He looks ahead rather than behind him. Lloyd seeks out novelty and new ways of thinking. His optimism and excitement are unequaled. An extrovert through and through, he fiercely fights off the dark moods that threaten to overtake his happiness. Lloyd is resilient. His perpetual and eternal self-confidence see him through the brooding storms of this life. His unshakable belief in victory originates from his very soul.

Todd is an esoteric dreamer and a screenwriter. He lives in worlds of chivalrous knights and frail damsels. However, despite his lavish imagination, Todd also is a practical man who lives in reality. He drives to Hollywood each week, and one can find him in countless background scenes as an "extra." Todd has no time for wishful thinking or waiting for luck to drop a leading role into his lap. He has no problem filling these smaller roles while relentlessly working his way up the ranks. The very personification of "tall, dark, and handsome," Todd's masculine virility and exceptional people skills will serve him well in his entertainment ambitions.

One brings up religion or politics at their own risk around this opinionated gentleman, who will promptly launch into a lofty speech. His audience seldom minds his moralizing, as his trustworthy friendship and loyalty are priceless. However, his sincerity and openheartedness have also worked against him, and Todd bears his share of rejection scars. He has learned to achieve equilibrium through "presence of mind," which allows him to handle all crises with diplomacy and restraint.

Both Lloyd and Todd have an unshakable confidence in their respective talents. Each will work their way up the political and social ladders to success. These two easily infatuated Horse souls are nonconformists, love social contact, and are never short on conversation. Constant stimulation in one form or another is essential to their emotional well-being. Both possess sharp, quick minds and intuitive abilities, and thrive in close contact with others.

The Goat/Sheep

The Creative Goat (Wei)— the "Capricious Artist"

February 13, 1907 to February 1, 1908: Fire Goat
February 1, 1919 to February 19, 1920: Earth Goat
February 17, 1931 to February 5, 1932: Metal Goat
February 5, 1943 to January 24, 1944: Water Goat
January 24, 1955 to February 11, 1956: Wood Goat
February 9, 1967 to January 29, 1968: Fire Goat
January 28, 1979 to February 15, 1980: Earth Goat
February 15, 1991 to February 3, 1992: Metal Goat
February 1, 2003 to January 21, 2004: Water Goat
February 19, 2015 to February 7, 2016: Wood Goat

Polarity: yin (negative)
Sign order: eighth
Alternate names: Sheep, Ram
Symbolism: proper timing, appropriateness
Lucky color: light green, chartreuse

Fragrance: orange bergmot
Flavor: sweet
Food/beverage: seafood, distilled spirits
Flower: delphinium, larspur
Gem: red carnelian, onyx
Feng shui direction: south/southwest
Lucky number: 12

This eighth position in the Chinese Zodiac, the Goat, is one of open possibilities, appropriate timing, and new beginnings. Those souls born into Goat years learn the lesson of "propriety"—they sense the correct time to act, employ moderation, and have an aversion to extremes. Goats are gentle and reflective, constructively applying their intelligence to the prevention of harm.

Goats are artists in both temperament and character. Those born into Goat years are animated, creative, and articulate. They are entertaining people who have many friends, some from very diverse walks of life. Goat souls will be found at social gatherings in the most breathtaking environments, engaged in stimulating conversation with extraordinarily fascinating people.

Sympathetic and honest, Goats are well-liked and known to be financially fortunate as long as they utilize their intuition and allow a more practical associate to take the helm. They often feel anxious, overwhelmed, and insecure, but have faith in their own intuition.

The most favorable time of day for the Goat is between 1 p.m. and 3 p.m., after a busy morning and a good lunch. This is the time when the yang power begins its decline and needs to be conserved by taking things slow and methodically. Work in the afternoon is more peaceful and productive for Goats than the morning hours, with their calls and crises. The Goat will gather energy during this afternoon period to carry them through the rest of the day.

Essential Temperament

Goats tend to rely on other people. They avoid conflicts and hate to be put face to face with responsibilities that they have no desire to assume. The sign of the Goat has universally represented abundance, an understanding nature, fertility, and new beginnings. Those born under this influence cannot live without beauty, and they strive for tranquility. They also don't appreciate having to choose sides between friends.

With strong spiritual leanings and an artistic flair, Goats are happier in a relaxed, creative environment. When something inspires a Goat, be it love, art, or a project, they are capable of almost anything. The easygoing Goat takes life at a slower pace than others. Goats are like strolling minstrels who roam freely through life, singing their own kind of song. This gentle soul is compassionate and loving, but tends toward moodiness and finds it difficult to work under pressure. The capriciousness of this sign is a Goat trademark. Goat people are some of the most changeable, yet creative, individuals around. A Goat will seem to float in and out of situations in life, changing the texture of the general mood by their presence alone. The Goat can vary its attention, starting one project, and then moving off to another, quickly and on a whim.

Goats have a reputation for numerous talents. While this versatility is an artistic blessing, if not channeled constructively, it can cause the Goat to be scattered. The Goat needs security and other people to depend on, and they desire to be looked after in loving, comfortable surroundings.

The Goat doesn't like schedules and never works well under pressure or hardship. The actors, artists, and musicians of this sign are known to exhibit a "garbage–in garbage out" syndrome. A disruptive environment or a heated argument will inhibit any creative effort and motivation. Goats are known to be adaptable and well mannered, but they mean what they say. Although they have a subdued outer appearance, the Goat can respond passionately and firmly. The pouty silence of a brooding Goat achieves more than angry words.

The Other Side—the Goat's Duality

In contrast to their many admirable attributes, unenlightened Goats can be irresponsible, undisciplined, and unreliable. An impulsive Goat can easily squander a small fortune or run up astronomical expenses. Dysfunctional Goats are dissatisfied, malcontent, and not good at making decisions. They prefer to be followers and will complain bitterly when matters don't go their way. Self-indulgent and inconsistent behavior represents the Goat's energy being directed in its most unproductive form. Expressed in its darkest form, this energy becomes extreme laziness, procrastination, dependence, pessimism, perpetual tardiness, and a victim mentality. The choice lies entirely with the individual. Taken to extreme, impulse control problems and obsessive-compulsive behavior may develop.

Gifts and Capabilities

Living in a world of whimsy and fantasy, the Goat prefers to avoid physically strenuous work. Being somewhat of an eccentric, Goats love the comfy life, and would do well to have an inheritance left to them. Early adulthood for this soul may be romantically stormy, but middle age and beyond is financially prosperous and lucky. According to Chinese tradition, the Goat will enjoy maturity, and in old age will want for nothing.

Two elemental qualities found in Goat-year souls are their peaceful and adaptable nature combined with an easygoing character. Personality weaknesses of the Goat include causing frustration or unnecessary delays, negative thinking, spending too much money, feeling dissatisfied, or being tardy. Happiness will come to the Goat when they are able to see through the ironies and contradictions of ordinary life and feel more confident in their own middle-of-the-road path.

Regarding health, Goat are delicate and susceptible to illness, being especially prone to diseases of the stomach and intestinal system. The ears, nose, and throat can also be problematic at times. To avoid illness Goats need plenty of sleep and should avoid too much exposure to the sun, because their skin is sensitive. Physical exercise should not be too demanding; instead, it should be moderate and enjoyable. Activities such as daily walking, gardening, dancing, and swimming are ideal to promote good health.

The Chinese believe that good fortune smiles on the Goat because of a pure nature and kind heart. Sometimes referred to as the

"Good Samaritans," Goat souls are generous with their time and financial resources. The Goat will rarely turn away a friend who needs food, shelter, or clothing. A person of this sign will make it a point to marry well and be cherished by their mate, as well as their in-laws. Goats attract favors from others, and their admirers enjoy presenting them with gifts and comfortable accommodations.

Goats are happiest and most fulfilled when their talents are appreciated. They crave love, attention, and approval in that order. The Goat will excel in any creative field where they have the freedom to work in a medium that inspires them. Goats have the soul of a connoisseur, and their mood is dependent on the environment. Beautiful environments are uplifting to them, but ugliness has a depressing effect.

The Child

Childhood is a precarious time for the Goat, and these children require harmony and security to thrive. Whimsical and insecure, these children need a realistic and solid ground to stand on. As a baby and youngster, the Goat child needs extra sleep to ensure strong health. Stock up on the crayons and paper, as the parent of a Goat child may have an artist on their hands. Inconsistent yet imaginative, Goat children excel in unstructured environments. Montessori schools are advantageous to Goat children. Goat children float from one project to the next and are wonderful friends and conversationalists. Getting to school on time can be a problem for Goats, as they cannot adhere to schedules and other people's time constraints.

Home and Hearth

The most favorable time of year for the Goat is between mid-August and mid-September, when the hot days alternate with cool, crisp nights; crops are harvested; and livestock begin to grow protective winter coverings. This is a time of celebration in China, as families gather together contemplating the abundance and beauty around them.

Auspicious Careers

The most harmonious career choices for Goats are those of artist, painter, stage/screen actor or actress, musician, landscape artist, weaver, or potter (all crafts). Intelligent, patient, and quiet, those born in the year of the Goat can fit into many different careers but will be happiest in the arts. As educators and medical professionals, the Goat shines. Sympathetic understanding combined with acute intelligence make them invaluable in these professions. Other favorable career choices include geologists, jewelers, dentists, chemists, veterinarians, scientists, programmers, fashion specialists, and public relations.

Neither especially active nor particularly ambitious, the Goat finds little value in the competitive spirit. It is a form of rivalry that will, in their eyes, involve them in conflicts and disputes. A spirit of "live and let live" will always be more important than the pursuit of power. This is not to say that Goats can bloom only in the arts; it's just that they will lack enthusiasm for other professions. Possessing a distaste for the mundane, the Goat is charming but "absent" behind a desk. Without an aesthetic or artistic contact, these souls wilt like plants deprived of water.

The Famous and the Infamous

Some famous and infamous Goats include: Bill Gates, Chow Yun-Fat, John Kerry, Pamela Anderson, Eva Peron, Oliver North, Kurt Cobain, Mick Jagger, Keith Richards, Mel Gibson, Bruce Willis, Julia Roberts, Goldie Hawn, Kate Hudson, William Shatner, Joe Pesci, Billy Bob Thornton, Hulk Hogan, Jim Jones, Billy Idol, Harry Connick Jr., George Harrison, Christopher Walken, Michelangelo, Winslow Homer, Franz Liszt, Grandma Moses, Liberace, Douglas Fairbanks, Rudolph Valentino, Sir Lawrence Olivier, Mark Twain,

George Burns, James Stewart, Newt Gingrich, Isaac Asimov, Lord Byron, Charles Dickens, Malcolm Forbes, Joni Mitchell, Debra Winger, and Barbara Walters.

Summary

Gentle Goat, when you're at your best you are a creative, artistic, and sympathetic soul. Through the ups and downs of this life, dear Goat, you will somehow always be fortunate and have things made easier for you. It is your karma born into this eighth sign of the Zodiac. At your worst, you can be brooding, emotional, and withdrawn. Avoid complaining when things do not meet your expectations. You share what you have with others, but you should be cautious that others don't take advantage of your generosity. We love your ability to create beauty and balance. Thank you for introducing us to the more pleasant sides of life. Many blessings, as you let your imagination soar!

The tide comes in tonight.
Once again, the sea of remembering
Calls me into nostalgic surf.
Waves of yesterday beckon me.
Hold my hand against this night;
Feed me warmth.
Together, let us count the stars.

The Goat Woman

When Sheri floats through a door, one is first struck by her grace and elegance. This gentle and feminine lady is enchantingly beautiful and has an aura of innocence surrounding her. Like her Horse sisters, Sheri loves to mix socially, enjoys great popularity, and is a favorite guest at any party. Her "live and let live" attitude relies on others for stability and support. Sheri, like many Goat women, has been fortunate financially. However, her handling of money has been nothing less than disastrous! Granted access to a large trust account at the young age of 18, Sheri embarked on a new career in "shopping." Now that she is older (and wiser) she has found an advocate to administer her estate, leaving Sheri free (and financially stable) to pursue her creative talents.

In the days when her bank account flowed freely, Sheri had many fair-weather friends who disappeared when the money ran dry. She has also been taken advantage of by several underhanded financial scams. But having a sympathetic and forgiving heart, Sheri considers spite, anger, and revenge to be useless and energy depleting. She reflects on the mistakes she has made, but doesn't dwell on the past. She looks optimistically forward to new pastures and firmly believes in the laws of karma.

Sheri is inspired by anything that brings harmony or adds beauty to her life. Her apartment is tastefully decorated with unusual color combinations and eccentric touches that just seem to "work." Carefree, easygoing, and a bit timid, she is a believer in compromise. Never one to deliberately antagonize another person, Sheri is a very intuitive soul and can sense things others cannot. More often than not, her hunches are right.

As mentioned earlier, she can be overly generous with others and tends to give whatever she has to anyone who touches her sympathies. She is an extraordinarily sensitive woman, and the sight of an injured or abandoned animal is almost unbearable for her. Sheri's sympathetic heart is concerned with the care of others, and she identifies with those less fortunate than herself.

Danielle has been blessed with a vivid imagination. Her portrait sketches look so realistic one would swear they could talk. She has a profoundly artistic and poetic soul. Possessing pronounced psychic ability, Danielle daydreams a lot, and she is an incurable romantic at heart. Danielle has struggled with her body image all of her life. She belongs unmistakably to the Rubenesque, well-curved, endomorphic group of women. She hates to sweat, and a regular exercise routine is torture for her. She prefers to spend her time relaxing, drawing, listening to music, or visiting with friends.

Physically, her resistance to viruses is low, and she is especially vulnerable to digestive ailments and intestinal troubles. She suffers from stomachaches, edema (due to a tendency to retain water), and endocrine/hormonal imbalances. She must avoid a high-carbohydrate, starchy diet as well as sweets and baked goods. Danielle needs more sleep than other women and, like her Rabbit sisters, her emotional stability depends on leading a quiet life. Meditation, t'ai chi, yoga, and qi gong would be very beneficial to her physical and emotional health.

Danielle has a tendency to be trusting, and she is vulnerable to the influences of others. Therefore, she must choose her companions wisely, as they have a great influence on her, for better or for worse. Despite her gentle and friendly manner, Danielle can capriciously switch into a completely different mindset. She has been known to be so focused on her own well-being and interests that she is unaware of her effect on others. At these times she does what she pleases, ignoring pressing responsibilities and procrastinating on urgent matters. Her moods can change rapidly, and she must resist the urge to escape harsh reality via medications or alcohol.

Danielle longs for a permanent romantic partner in her life, but her behavior shows some contradictions. She is very picky in her choice of men, and while pursued by many, she only has eyes for the unattainable ones. On one hand, she wants an ideal union of comfort and ease; on the other hand, she is fearful of being hurt, or worse, left poverty stricken and alone. She does like children, but a house filled with crying, demanding babies is certainly not for her. She loves her art and is truly a genius with it. Her creative projects bring her joy and satisfaction, yet she fears tainting it with pressure, which would surely result from making it a full-time profession. Almost always, she displays more talent than efficiency.

Both of these good-natured ladies must attach themselves to a strong support system capable of encouraging them to cultivate their capabilities.

The Goat Man

Being of the yin, night-force disposition, Nathaniel is motivated by his feelings and perceptions. Not at all combative, Nathaniel is a lover, not a fighter.

His easygoing attitude is sometimes viewed as apathetic but, in actuality, he is very much engaged and merely lost in his own inner world. Like his Goat sisters, Nathaniel is an artistic, creative, and romantic soul. He thinks in abstract terms, and his strong intuition allows him to comprehend even the most obscure concepts. Not surprisingly, he is a spiritual advisor and well versed in all manner of metaphysics. This master of the esoteric has an extraordinary gift for counseling and the intricacies of the human mind. He works in a resident home for emotionally disturbed children.

Nathaniel's self-esteem is closely tied to his capacity for empathy. Extremely sensitive to the feelings and emotions of other people, he always lends a patient and empathetic ear to the troubles and concerns of others. His compassionate heart has difficulty accepting man's inhumanity to man, and it is difficult for him to see pain and cruelty. He is a soul who will do everything in his power to help those in distress.

Nathaniel's health is as fragile as his Goat sisters. He should avoid exposure to illness and practice preventive care as much as possible. Digestive difficulties plague him, and he has suffered from stomach ulcers. Moderation in all things should be his motto. Violent contact sports are absolutely not advised, but swimming and all water-based sports are beneficial for him.

Despite being competent to counsel, Nathaniel is deeply dependent on positive emotional support from others. During his occasional dark moods, he suffers from self-doubts and sometimes feels inadequate. Like his Dog-year brothers, he is much harsher on himself than any critic could ever be. He has wisely surrounded himself with supportive and encouraging friends. Almost exclusively ruled by his feelings, Nathaniel maneuvers through life with his hand on the pulse of society. He fulfills his karmic Goat-year purpose as the spiritual barometer of the Eastern Zodiac.

Mark is the personification of a modern rock star. His only truth is what he feels at any given moment. Fantastically successful by the world's standards, Mark suffers from dissatisfaction with life. He is frequently bored and often at the mercy of his moods, which are changeable and unpredictable. Mark is inconsistent, unreliable, and not punctual. He describes himself as "always late, but worth the wait."

While undeniably self-indulgent, Mark is accepting of others and never condemns those who are different from himself. In fact, he celebrates diversity and prides himself on having friends from diverse walks of life. He is fascinated by human behavior and possesses keen insights into the motivations of others. Mark is an intuitive pacifist to his very core and was a card-carrying member, so to speak, of the 1960s "make love not war" alliance.

At heart, he detests violence of every description, never deliberately doing anyone harm or flaming up in a stormy temper, and often allows himself to be pushed around by others without resistance. While not particularly demanding, he is ever willing to lend a helping hand, and many people feel relieved to entrust him with their secrets. He is a gentle and charming soul who is moved by a sincere and profound desire to give pleasure. Few can remain insensitive to his sweetness, courtesy, and pleasantness. He is accommodating to the point of being apologetic.

Although possessing a distinct stage persona, he is always true to himself. He laughs at his various imperfections and has no need to flaunt his accomplishments. Mark functions best as part of a team effort, and his noncompetitive spirit needs and appreciates those who willingly take the lead. His sense of beauty and discrimination has naturally led him into the arts. Original and imaginative, Mark has music in his very soul.

Both men's essence of propriety urges them to hesitate before acting, to always consider protocol, and to act in an appropriate manner. Far from dysfunctional dreamers, both Nathaniel and Mark are traveling troubadours through this life. Their intuitive decisions most often turn out to be the right ones, and both men have the ability to predict an outcome from its very beginning.

The Monkey

The Entertaining Monkey (Shen)— the "Merry Mercurial"

February 2, 1908 to January 21, 1909: Earth Monkey
February 20, 1920 to February 7, 1921: Metal Monkey
February 6, 1932 to January 25, 1933: Water Monkey
January 25, 1944 to February 12, 1945: Wood Monkey
February 12, 1956 to January 30, 1957: Fire Monkey
January 30, 1968 to February 16, 1969: Earth Monkey
February 16, 1980 to February 4, 1981: Metal Monkey
February 4, 1992 to January 22, 1993: Water Monkey
January 22, 2004 to February 8, 2005: Wood Monkey
February 8, 2016 to January 27, 2017: Fire Monkey

Polarity: yang (positive)
Sign order: ninth
Symbolism: unhindered mind
Lucky colors: orange, violet
Fragrance: ylang-ylang
Flavor: spicy, ripe
Flower: poppy

Food/beverage: gourmet cuisine, burgundy/merlot
Gem: sardonyx
Feng shui direction: west-southwest
Lucky number: 10

The ninth position in the Chinese Zodiac, the Monkey, is one of action, possibilities, and remarkable energy. Those souls born into Monkey years learn the lesson of "irrepressibility." Monkeys are clever, mentally quick, and exceedingly resourceful.

Those born into Monkey years are also smart and inventive thinkers. They love to learn and are blessed with an excellent memory. Monkeys are warm and confident, but can become easily sidetracked. They possess a mercurial temperament that allows them to streamline any task. Efficient, they are always able to figure out an easier way to get the job done.

The term "hyperactive" is sometimes used when discussing those born in Monkey years. They have the ability to get tremendous amounts done in almost no time at all. Monkeys also can maneuver their way out of all kinds of dilemmas. They use this innate cunning to achieve goals and squeeze out of all manner of sticky situations. Their charm and curiosity keep them going. Monkeys cannot stand boredom, ill will, or rejection. Monkey-year souls are competitive yet jovial companions. They are popular and optimistic with almost everyone, and have a myriad of interests in life.

Favorable hours of the day for Monkeys fall between 3 p.m. and 5 p.m., when the sun is still shining and the yin force is gathering its energy. This is the time of day when Monkeys are effervescent with energy.

Essential Temperament

Monkeys are cerebral. They need to be stimulated and teased mentally before their interest is aroused. Witty jokes, yarns, and other assorted comedic gems flow naturally and freely from Monkey souls. It is generally agreed that both male and female Monkeys tend to be funny. Their sarcastic simian wit, combined with perfect timing, make them enjoyable and refreshing partners. If there is a problem to be solved, the Monkey is the one who is competent to counsel on resolving the dilemma.

Of all of the 12 signs, the Monkey is the one with the most multicolored nature. Mischievous and high-spirited, Monkeys are enterprising and outgoing, and make an instant connection with just about everyone. This allows them tremendous success in any profession where sales, persuasion, and cunning are required.

Monkeys need movement, discussion, and the retort of ideas. They cheerfully care for others who are down on their luck, and are unrivaled at simplifying and solving problems. The Monkey fears being excluded or ignored and is sorely stung by the barb of indifference. This shakes their confidence and is one of the few things that can send them into depression. Favorite leisure activities are, not surprisingly, social ones, and Monkeys like to circulate in diverse circles. Reunions, parties, and the local pub are favorite mingling spots. Anywhere the Monkey can communicate and make merry.

Curious, crafty, and an excellent student, higher learning for Monkeys is almost effortless. Monkeys adapt marvelously to diverse lifestyles and often have a gift for languages. Surprises and good friends constitute heaven on earth for these social souls. It is important for Monkeys to balance their perpetual energy and curb suspicions regarding the motives of others. Accelerated mental thought can lead to obsessions and compulsions. Enlightened Monkeys will learn to manage and channel their intrinsically high activity levels into productive and benevolent acts.

The Other Side—the Monkey's Duality

In contrast to their many admirable attributes, unenlightened Monkeys can be opportunistic and status seeking. The complex Monkey nature may also hide a low opinion and secret distrust of other people.

Suspicious and arrogant behavior represents the Monkey's energy being directed in its most unproductive form. When the Monkey's complicated and dubious personality becomes skewed, serious interpersonal problems can occur and maintaining relationships of long duration proves impossible. Expressed in its darkest form, this energy becomes trickery, infidelity, vanity, distrust, self-interest, and immature behavior. The choice lies completely with the individual. Taken to extreme, paranoid and anti-social personality disorders may develop.

Gifts and Capabilities

Monkeys enjoy an unquenchable thirst for the fountain of knowledge. They read books, magazines, and newspapers, eager to be briefed and up to date on current affairs. Well-bred and well-educated, the Monkey has the closest thing to a photographic memory of all the animal signs. While blessed with many wonderful attributes, it is within the Monkey's original and inventive mind and impeccable sense of humor that we find the essence of this soul.

The best role for a Monkey is that of persuader, innovator, or personal assistant and advisor to royalty. International travel pleases the restless Monkey's soul, and many choose careers as airline pilots, flight attendants, or travel agents. Where assets are concerned, Monkeys are financially lucky and will receive handsome rewards due to their ingenuity and personal charm. However, funds available are funds to be spent for enjoyment and pleasure.

The Child

As a child, the Monkey will "never walk if they can run." Indeed, those parents blessed with Monkey children may want to purchase a pair of roller skates to keep up with these mischievous little scamps. Full of fun and fantasy, this intelligent and personable child makes friends easily and will display an extraordinary sense of humor at an early age. Practical jokes are a specialty of Monkey children, and no sign is as proficient in fooling, tricking, and enchanting others.

Monkey children often disassemble, reassemble, deconstruct, and reconstruct their environment. Discarded logs become boats, fabric scraps become quilts, and radios get disassembled to see how they work. These Peter Pan and "Panettes" of the Zodiac seldom completely grow up, and their soul remains eternally youthful.

Home and Hearth

Monkey parents prefer to have more of a friendship with their children than a parental dictatorship. They make sure their children have stimulating, fun opportunities to discover, experience, and enjoy. Monkeys tend to have difficulty being firm with their offspring and prefer to reinforce positive behavior using rewards rather than via fear of punishment. Convinced of the inherent goodness in humans, Monkey parents are broad-minded, tolerant, and fair. They assist their children on the journey to discover their own identities and self-confidence. Abhorring stringent controls themselves, Monkey parents are flexible and maintain a low-key home life. The most favorable time of year for Monkeys is from mid-September to mid-October, when the seasons change and life begins its preparation for the long winter.

Auspicious Careers

Monkeys are so multitalented that they have an excellent chance of succeeding in any career field. Monkeys do best, however, in positions that demand a high degree of specialty and require creative freedom. Contributing to society and making tangible progress is important to them no matter what the profession. Monkeys specialize in complex tasks and will always rise to the top of their fields. Many filmmakers, screenwriters, and performers were born into Monkey years. Monkey souls are natural comedians, and they are the kings and queens of stand-up comedy. They also make shrewd politicians and are master manipulators (if they so choose). With a natural bent for problem-solving, Monkeys also make excellent business advisors and troubleshooters. Their love of travel can place them in careers such as airline pilots, flight attendants, and travel agents. On the other side of the fence, Monkeys have also been known to pursue careers as confidence men, professional gamblers, and unscrupulous outlaws.

The Famous and the Infamous

Some famous and infamous Monkeys include Jennifer Aniston, Lucy Liu, Will Smith, Dana Delany, Tom Hanks, Gillian Anderson, Tom Selleck, Patricia Arquette, Michael Douglas, Chelsea Clinton, Danny DeVito, Patti LaBelle, Jerry Springer, Ricki Lake, Jerry Hall, Glenn Gould, Elizabeth Taylor, Donald Rumsfeld, Macaulay Culkin, Harry Houdini, Little Richard, Johnny Cash, Ted Kennedy, Eleanor Roosevelt, Alice Walker, Martina Navratilova, Delta Burke, Andy Garcia, J.M. Barrie, David Copperfield, Joe Cocker, Bette Davis, Julius Caesar, Milton, Byron, Charles Dickens, Buster Keaton, Frederico Fellini, Rex Harrison, Susan B. Anthony, Annie Oakley, and the Marquis de Sade.

Summary

Mischievous Monkey, one never knows what new idea or project you have brewing in that bright mind of yours, but count us in! It is said, "read 10,000 books and walk 10,000 miles." Studying books will enlarge your secondhand knowledge, but it is only through a hands-on, observational approach that you will enrich your first-hand knowledge. Combining past and present wisdom with practical experience is the path to enlightenment for you. Resist questioning other's motives, for suspicion saps your spirit. Come from a position of strength and trust in your own good karma. As an extraordinary collaborator and partner in crime, we look to you to decipher our dilemmas, solve our situations, and help us maneuver around our impasses. Preserve your precious energy, which *is* (contrary to popular belief) exhaustible.

We have both known the winter.
I would have you stay with me
In the warmth of my summer sun;
But you have yet to touch
The new green leaves of your spring.

The Monkey Woman

When Laura enters a room she brings many women with her. She is a multifaceted soul containing multiple personas and paradoxes. Alternating between innuendo and candor, flexibility and stubbornness, Laura is a kaleidoscope of impulses, emotions, and opinions. This extraordinary woman seeks to expand her knowledge base and stimulate her razor-sharp mind.

Romantically, Laura has experienced a tug-of-war between her intellect and her emotions. While she had no difficulty acquiring a Ph.D., this brilliant soul has had more difficulty in finding true love. She will admit that her head and her heart rarely agree. She may have strong feelings for someone and, at the same time, be entertaining suspicions that make her skeptical about the relationship.

This "sentimental duality" has been the source of internal struggle for Laura. It is the main reason behind her change of heart when her partner's shortcomings begin to surface. Restrained and excitable, Laura consciously tries to keep a sensible balance between her cerebral needs and her emotional desires.

Laura enjoys good health, but her physical soundness is closely tied to her serenity, or lack thereof. Her inner nervousness and an inability to "turn her mind off" have caused her many sleepless nights. She wisely knows that pharmaceuticals are not the answer; instead, she exercises daily and strictly limits her caffeine intake. As a child, Laura contracted polio. This left her legs partially paralyzed, requiring her to use crutches and undergo numerous surgeries. Years of physical therapy and an irrepressible "can-do" attitude has brought her back to almost complete mobility. Laura, like many Monkey women, contends with various skeletal problems, from simple curvature of the spine to more serious loss of motion.

Whether bringing hot soup to locked-out strikers walking the picket lines or participating in a political protest, Marie is present and accounted for. Always actively involved in some manner, and at times radically struggling against the powers that be, Marie stands up for causes she believes in and people for whom she cares.

Hers is a soul that challenges out-of-date, arbitrary rules and dictatorial regulations. Her numerous crusades are waged because she earnestly wants to make this world a better place. She is an idealist by nature, but is also intellectually shrewd and blessed with penetrating powers of perception. Marie can untangle even the most complicated of problems.

Seeking to improve mankind, Marie is an idealist who believes her cup to be half full rather than half empty. Unorthodox at times, her encouragement and friendship endear her to others and she is a fun and helpful sidekick.

Developing new ways of nonconformity is mental exercise for Marie. Novelty, innovation, and those things that lie ahead are the subjects that interest her. Change doesn't frighten her; in fact, it energizes her. She assimilates and assesses everything in her environment so quickly that she bores rapidly. Marie is an interesting and diverse woman who wants to uncover new information, design fascinating inventions, and discover the way to never-never land.

Marie is highly creative and original. She is a talented and successful writer of grant proposals that request funds for worthy projects and studies. She is at her best when involved in activities that allow her to defend a just cause, preferably a revolutionary one.

In romance, Marie is skeptical of strong emotions, yet secretly dreams of the magical kiss that will awaken her, and of the handsome lord who delivers it. But alas, reality invades her fantasy. This is a woman who must partner with a man who is her complete intellectual equal. Contradictions abound, and her unpredictability is a part of her charm. For her, romance must begin with mutual admiration and respect.

Both Laura and Marie are clever and charming Monkey women. Each is proficient in self-preservation, extremely versatile, and no challenge is too great for either of them to conquer. They are gregarious, humorous, and friendly, yet trust very few people in this life. Each woman triumphs over life through her intelligence and everlasting enthusiasm.

The Monkey Man

Tommy is a rebel and a rascal. His eyes twinkle with mischief and he can always be counted on to be the life of the party. He has been blessed with an active imagination and a hilarious sense of humor. An extraordinary storyteller and master "yarn-spinner," Tommy writes children's books and has twice received the prestigious Caldecott. Being a child at heart, Tommy understands and speaks a child's language of idealism and innocence.

Beneath Tommy's animated smile exists a man who can tolerate just about anything except a lack of interest. Being his own employer gives him the flexibility and room for originality that drives his creativity. Insomnia can be a problem for him, and he wisely uses meditation and music to relax his active mind. While possessing the semblance of simplicity, Tommy is an extremely complicated individual.

It is in his love life that Tommy's complex personality plays the most noticeable role. Capriciously vacillating between "he loves me" and "he loves me not," Tommy is uncertain if he will ever relinquish his freedom to marriage. On the other hand, his heart overflows with sentiment and he has no desire to be a hermit. More infatuations than serious interest, Tommy's relationships have not progressed far.

While unquestionably cerebral, he experiences life on a heart level. Unable to tolerate any restrictions on his independence, Tommy rejects antiquated social graces and battles against authority. Akin to his otherworldly Dragon brothers, Tommy's interest in the future and fascination with the concept of utopia is a large part of his charm.

As a confirmed individualist and eccentric, Tommy keeps his own counsel and follows his own set of rules. A fan of novelty and the unorthodox, he is not a judgmental person. He is the very personification of the "pioneer," tearing down and rebuilding anew. He forages for spiritual nutrients in unexplored realms.

Dennis possesses a sixth sense regarding human nature. This has unfortunately moved him into a skeptical mind-set in love. His need for variety and insatiable curiosity have derailed several serious relationships with infidelities, and the loss is obvious. Dennis admits to being lonely at times, but he enjoys an upbeat life and is an avid fisherman. He has several close friends and never misses placing a bet on his favorite sports teams. Oddly enough, some of Dennis's closest platonic "buddies" are women. Chauvinism isn't in this man's vocabulary, and he amiably remains on friendly terms, even with ex-partners.

Dennis's most invaluable gift is his earthy common sense. When it comes to versatility, there is none better, and his cleverness is apparent in his hobbies. Dennis is a weekend tool warrior. Armed with hammer and saw, boards and nails, he proceeds to construct a perfectly professional patio. This talented handyman combines both ingenuity and usability. Few know that he was an honor student and has an impressive collection of diplomas displayed on his home office wall.

Routine and boredom are akin to a prison cell for this high-functioning man. Dennis, like many Monkey men, embodies the image of the international bachelor playboy. Seeing himself as a forthright person, he makes no apologies for his lifestyle and cares nothing about traditional social mores. This isn't a man who requests permission from society for anything

Similar to his Monkey brother Tommy, Dennis doesn't always put his cards on the table. He can be patronizing, telling others what he thinks they want to hear. Dennis optimistically believes that with every crisis there is offered both danger and opportunity. Life's challenges generally do not deter him, nor does he indulge in pity parties.

He firmly believes that no matter how bad today has been, there will always be a better tomorrow.

Both Tommy and Dennis are good-natured, kind, and above all, firm believers in the human dignity of every person. Each man travels in the liveliest social circles and has friends from divergent backgrounds. These mischievous Monkey men teach others to see the humor in life and preach the healing power of laughter.

Chapter 12

The Rooster

The Perfectionistic Rooster (You)— the "I Can Do Better Inspirer"

January 22, 1909 to February 9, 1910: Earth Rooster
February 8, 1921 to January 27, 1922 : Metal Rooster
January 26, 1933 to February 13, 1934: Water Rooster
February 13, 1945 to February 1, 1946 : Wood Rooster
January 31, 1957 to February 17, 1958: Fire Rooster
February 17, 1969 to February 5, 1970 : Earth Rooster
February 5, 1981 to January 24, 1982: Metal Rooster
January 23, 1993 to February 9, 1994: Water Rooster
February 9, 2005 to January 28, 2006: Wood Rooster
January 28, 2017 to February 15, 2018: Fire Rooster

Polarity: yin (negative)
Sign order: 10th
Alternate name: Cock, Hen
Lucky colors: Jewel tones, turquoise, fuschia
Fragrance: gardenia, star jasmine

Flavor: spicy
Food/beverage: fruits, nuts, carbonated beverages
Flower: aster
Gem: sapphire
Feng shui direction: west
Lucky number: six

This tenth position in the Chinese Zodiac, the Rooster, is one of attention, observance, and scrutiny. Those souls born into Rooster years learn the lesson of "application": the ability to utilize, apply, and practice mundane activities, realizing delayed gratification. Roosters look to future goals, watching their hard work accrue rewards. The Rooster works with great determination, keeping their eyes ever forward on the goal.

Roosters are brave and confident in work and in life. They are hardworking, cautious, and critical. A Rooster doesn't mince words and can verbally shoot from the hip. Often brilliant, they are at their best in a crowded room, and shine more in company than in intimate situations. The Rooster loves to dream and meditate upon grandiose ideas and philosophies. In Asain tradition, it is said that the Rooster is so resourceful they "can find a worm in a desert!" This explains the continual and restless activity that characterizes this sign.

The personality of those born under the sign of the Rooster consists of three levels: appearance, practicality, and strong emotion. Roosters are generally well-dressed, and an observer is often struck first by their elegant gestures and rich colors. These souls rarely pass unnoticed. Scrupulous about their appearance, a Rooster will become ruffled at others lack of taste, and are never completely satisfied with their own look even though they seem quite self-confident.

The most favorable hours of the day for the Rooster are between 5 p.m. and 7 p.m., the last yang hours of the day, when the setting sun radiates its most glorious colors. For the Rooster, who was the first to greet the day, and has been dilligently at work ever since, it is the time to relax and enjoy these pre-evening hours.

Essential Temperament

The Rooster is pure-minded and hates hypocrisy. They are discriminating critics, and their life-creed is "I can do better." This is because Roosters acomplish things quicker and more efficiently than most. Their criticism and cynical observations will just be factual statements to them, and they have no intention of offending you personally. A Rooster simply must speak their mind and is a truly independent spirit.

During the four stages in the life of the Rooster, according to Chinese tradition, there will be many ups and downs. From childhood, through youth and maturity, the Rooster is the sign with the greatest joys and the deepest sorrows. They are sometimes rich, sometimes poor, sometimes surrounded by friends, and sometimes alone. According to Chinese tradition, emotional stability will be attained as the Rooster becomes settled in a profession or identity, and the Rooster will enjoy a happy and contented old age.

Roosters are adaptable, which helps them to feel at home just about anywhere. If you wish to give your Rooster a gift, remember that it is the feeling that counts to them, so you can't go wrong when you choose something that comes from your heart.

The Other Side—the Rooster's Duality

In contrast to their many admirable attributes, unenlightened Roosters can be vain, hairsplitting, and hypercritical. The shadow side of the Rooster is egotism. They focus on perfection and are highly critical of others as they hurl their caustic comments. Sarcastic and harsh behavior represents the Rooster's energy being directed in its most unproductive form. Expressed in its darkest form, this energy becomes manic-depressive, caustic, pompous, tactless, preoccupied with appearance, suspicious, or braggart behavior. The choice lies entirely with the individual. Taken to extreme, manic depression and sadistic personality disorders may develop.

Gifts and Capabilities

Roosters are highly cultivated and, beneath their cordial manner, capable of serious conversation. Having read a great deal, they are knowledgeable about a large variety of subjects and possess an excellent memory. Curiously, however, they rarely display this knowledge openly. Roosters reveal themselves only to their family and intimate friends, as they fear being the subject of a gossip session. A Rooster resists any attempt from outsiders to probe their private being or expose their personal business.

Roosters are charming, but they are also sometimes difficult to live with due to their tireless work ethic and preoccupation with the here and now. If a Rooster seems indifferent to the state of mind of others, it is with innocence and good faith, as they are merely distracted and following their own route and routine.

This same Rooster can always be counted on during times of disaster and dire necessity. When you are sick with the flu and the plumbing has backed up, the Rooster will appear with medicine and tools to restore order in record time.

Regarding money, the Rooster can be extravagant and often has a hard time resisting temptation. However, many Roosters are financially fortunate due to their motto of "never put off for tomorrow what you can do today," and their karmic gift to tolerate deferred gratifcation.

The Child

As children, Roosters are usually ahead of their peers in academics and are known to have little tolerance for messiness and sloppiness, both mentally and practically. Many a mother of a Rooster child has asked herself, "Who is the parent here?" as the young Rooster instructs the parent on the proper way to do things. A Rooster is uncomfortable in a messy house or cluttered work area. They give of themselves completely in all work endeavors; therefore, these souls need leisure activities and evenings spent socializing or reading to unwind.

Home and Hearth

Favorite places for the Rooster are private corners of their own, where others can enter by invitation only—a kind of "secret garden." Harmonious colors are violet, yellow, and green. Medicinal plants and flowers for them are gentian, orange and palm trees, sunflowers, and hawthorn. Their natal birthstone is the topaz.

The most favorable time of year for the Rooster is between mid-October and mid-November, when the harvest is ending and Chinese people are at their happiest, seeing the reward of so much labor. For the Rooster, who works so diligently throughout the year, this is a most bountiful and rewarding time. The Rooster, who feels like the host of the harvest celebration, can then break their tedious routine and pause to take pride in their achievements and successes.

Auspicious Careers

The best role for a Rooster is that of a collector, accountant, or financier, and as the "hero" of difficult projects. The worst role for the Rooster is that of a spy (much too conspicuous). Any commercial profession, from salesperson to head sales manager, will also be a good fit. Military officer/soldier, fireman, restaurant/cafe owner, high-fashion hairdresser, model, public relations specialist, dentist, surgeon, and bodyguard will also provide positive career alternatives for Roosters. An outstanding performer, this animal sign shines when they are the center of attention. Full-fledged as a personality, the Rooster could well pursue any career that is in the public eye. Joyful, witty, and amusing, the magnificent Rooster will rarely pass up the opportunity to recount their adventures and accomplishments. This makes them ideally suited to the performing arts, and many accomplished actors, actresses, as well as frontline fighters are found under this sign.

The Famous and the Infamous

Some famous and infamous Roosters include Renee Zellweger, Chris Carter, Michelle Pfeiffer, LeVar Burton, Melanie Griffith, Deborah Harry, Dean Koontz, Nancy Kerrigan, Dolly Parton, Rudyard Kipling, Enrico Caruso, Groucho Marx, Ethel Merman, Stephen Foster, Eric Clapton, Joan Collins, Gloria Estefan, Errol Flynn, Richard Harris, Steffi Graf, Larry King, Yoko Ono, Nancy Reagan, Benjamin Franklin, Johann Strauss, Catherine the Great, Brigham Young, the Duke of Marlborough, Peter Ustinov, Katharine Hepburn, Debra Kerr, William Faulkner, Marian Anderson, Prince Philip, Osama Bin Laden, Neil Young, Willie Nelson, George Segal, Joan Rivers, Carol Burnett, Steve Martin, Van Morrison, and Bette Midler.

Summary

Proud Rooster, your tireless energy is amazing. Some who don't know you well may call you arrogant, but we who know you, know better. That saucy self-reliance is just an outward shell concealing a kind, conservative, and family-oriented soul. A good provider and wonderful to your family, we salute your common sense and efficiency. Relax and let your hair down once in a while. Also, remember that the spectators see more of the game than the players. Ask others for their point of view, as onlookers have a calmer and more objective perspective. We will only think the better of you for it!

Darkness veils
Natures rich regalia.
Sunlight hides
The crown jewels of a Universe.

The Rooster Woman

Margie is a woman who is either hot or cold, but never lukewarm. Despite her petite physical stature, her magnatism and intense presence are 6 feet tall. She has the power to bewitch and hold others spellbound. "Come into my parlor, said the spider to the fly," is the attraction (with reservations) aura that Margie exudes. But this femme fatale is fully aware of her disquieting demeanor.

Her voice is sensual and deep. Her striking auburn hair is piled high atop her head and at times resembles a crest. Margie is the mother of five daughters and is a strict disciplinarian. She is also highly conscientious and fiercely protective of her children. Through the scrapes and scuffles of childhood, Margie's maternal advice to her girls has always been, "bullies will push you as far as you let them."

Blessed with good health and inexaustible energy, Margie pushes the limits of her emotional and physical endurance to the point of being self-destructive at times. She is a soul who leans toward the extreme ends of life and has little understanding of the middle road.

As a result of her extreme nervous tensions, Margie often suffers from headaches, but even these seldom slow her down. She also has a tendency to punish herself with strict diets and stringent routines. Margie is sharp, direct, and has a will of iron. Not predisposed to compromise, she staunchly defends her views and opinions. She also possesses a natural authority and others rarely oppose her.

Charming and friendly on the surface, she keeps her aggresive tendencies under tight rein. She prefers to entice rather than repel others into doing her bidding.

Harnessing her intensity and controling her deep-seated anxiety is a formidable obstacle for Margie. Looking back, she regrets past rages and emotional eruptions of volcanic proportions. When provoked, she is capable of hurling caustic criticisms, which burn like acid and disfigure the smiles of those around her. Brutal truths spill from her when disappointed or opposed.

However, when the storm clouds clear, Margie returns to her talkative, enchanting self. Blessed with a high intelligence, her judgement is sound and practical. She has a talent for cutting to the chase and sifting through word-fodder to discover the truth in every situation. Her gaze is penetrating and direct, revealing a soul who is serious and has difficulty laughing at herself.

If advice is what you seek, Margie is the woman to see. Her deeply conservative "yin" nature has workable solutions for any problem. While tact and compromise are not in her vocabulary, she is gifted at managing money, is a perfectionist in everything she does, and is always a tireless worker.

Cheryl, like her Rooster sister Margie, has difficulty channeling her overwhelming energy. Capable of great achievements in this life, she has chosen to harness her spunk as a communications specialist in the United States Air Force. The disciplined lifestyle, combined with the sense of pride and patriotism inherent in the military, provides the perfect stage for Cheryl to showcase her motivation and efficiency. Cheryl also has a fascination for perilous situations and risk. She has found a rewarding career through which she can flex her muscles and fight against fate itself.

Difficulties, obstacles, and adversity bring out the best in both Margie and Cheryl. There is no challenge too great for these two efficient souls to undertake. While occasionally the "end can justify the means" in their eyes, these curious Rooster ladies yearn to investigate and discover the mysteries and meanings of life itself. Passionate, strong-willed, and self-confident, both women need a strong partner whom they can admire unconditionally; one who will stand his ground, is equally as capable as she is, and who is willing to playfully spar with them verbally. For those whom they love and respect, both Margie and Cheryl are sentimental, as well as loyal companions.

The Rooster Man

Erich has the focused intensity of a laser beam. His manerisms are restless, and his speech effusive and direct. He possesses a vital life force and is very much the master of his own destiny. As a mechanical engineer, no detail escapes his attention, and his perfectionism is evident in everything he does. When life is on the upswing, Erich is a charming and well-mannered gentleman. However, if frustrated or challenged he will quickly become inflexibile and indignant. Holding ironclad convictions, Erich cannot tolerate criticism and is indifferent to opposing opinions.

Erich is a soul who moves from life's mountaintops to the depths of its valleys with regularity. Karmicly destined to be a man of extremes, Erich does nothing half-heartedly. He is firmly convinced that he knows what is best, not only for himself but for others as well. He is never wishy-washy and always takes a clear-cut, definitive stand on any issue.

Ultra-conservative in love, Erich keeps a tight control over his emotions and never trusts them completely. He is reserved, and often hesitates to reveal his true emotions. He takes himself and his commitments very seriously and is a faithful husband. After many disapointments in love, Erich has found a life-partner who sincerely understands his fears, hopes, disapointments, and dreams. He considers himself a lucky man. While a house full of rowdy offspring was not high on his life agenda, now that he has two precocious children, he is a devoted albeit strict father.

The greatest danger to his health is his bipolar emotions, which can hold him hostage. When manic, he will not stop or slow down; when depressed, he suffers from painful stress-related headaches that can imobilize him. His physical well-being is joined at the hip to his emotional state. Any illness is exacerbated by his tightly strung nervous system and nagging anxieties.

Personally, Erich is not an easy man to get to know. He often conceals his inner world, jealously guarding his intentions and vulnerabilities. His secretiveness originates from his deep suspicions of others and fear of interference in his affairs. Erich has been blessed with a penetrating intelligence. His mind is skeptical, cautious, shrewd, and quick-witted. He can instinctually sense the soft underside of his enemies and locks in on the weaknesses of his competition. Erich possesses the mind and soul of a four-star military strategist.

Although Dan is only in his early 20s, he views life soberly and allows himself very little "wiggle room." This serious, young man has concrete goals that he fully intends to reach. Dan is practical and levelheaded, looks at life squarely, and has no illusions. He confines his thinking to the tested and the concrete. His luck tends to move in waves, bringing inevitable ups and downs in life.

Dan's appearance is very important to him, and he is always impeccably groomed. Like all good Roosters, he enjoys being the center of attention, struting his assets and preening his handsome feathers. He adores being center stage, interacts best in a group, and is quick to point out his many talents. Humility and self-effacement are foreign concepts to him, but Dan's profound loyalty and sense of personal honor endear him to others. Too proud to ask for help himself, Dan is always available when others need his assistence. When a friend was stranded by the side of the road with a disabled vehicle, Dan was quickly enroute with jack and tools in hand. When an untimely skiing accident temporarily incapacitated another close friend, Dan took care of paying his hospital bills and completed urgent household repairs for him.

Dan's life motto is one of "absolute victory." Success and opportunities for self-mastery are what interest him. Like his Rooster brother Erich, Dan is efficient and applies himself fully. Possessing the courage of a firefighter, the discipline of an officer, and the appearence of a movie star, Dan has every chance to see his dreams become a reality.

Both Erich and Dan have choosen to work within the highest vibrations of their Rooster birth year and channel their intense energies into creative and productive projects. Both men are emotionally high-strung and must continually contend with inner frustrations. Those who know and love them understand their psychology, and reliably provide encouragement and reassurance.

Chapter 13

The Dog

The Watchful Dog (Xu)— the "Vanquishing Vigilante"

February 10, 1910 to January 29, 1911: Metal Dog
January 28, 1922 to February 15, 1923: Water Dog
February 14, 1934 to February 3, 1935: Wood Dog
February 2, 1946 to January 21, 1947: Fire Dog
February 18, 1958 to February 7, 1959: Earth Dog
February 6, 1970 to January 26, 1971: Metal Dog
January 25, 1982 to February 12, 1983: Water Dog
February 10, 1984 to January 30, 1995: Wood Dog
January 29, 2006 to February 3, 2007: Fire Dog
February 16, 2018 to February 4, 2019: Earth Dog

Polarity: yang (positive)
Sign order: 11th
Symbolism: frontline of battle
Lucky color: indigo blue
Fragrance: balsam, musk
Flavor: rich, buttery

Food/beverage: red meat, cheese, milk
Flower: orange blossom, tea rose
Gem: opal
Feng shui direction: west-northwest
Lucky number: nine

The 11th position in the Chinese Zodiac, the Dog, is one of extreme loyalty toward those whom they love and intense ferocity toward their loved one's enemies. Those souls born into Dog years learn the lesson of "watchfulness"—the ability to mix alertness and quiet caution with great boldness when defending or protecting those under their care.

Quartered between tradition and rebellion, the Dog soul personifies some of the most altruistic traits of human nature. Loyal, dependable, and unselfish, a Dog never turns their back on a friend. Any unfairness sends them into "battle mode," and Dogs consider it a personal mission to correct the wrongdoings of others. Where there is disaster and human suffering, Dogs are always on the front line. With their feet firmly planted, the diffident Dog protests any inequities and strives to correct injustices.

At their happiest when they have a humanitarian purpose, the Dog is principled, trustworthy, nonmaterialistic, and has a strong sense of right and wrong. Those souls born into a year of the Dog make lifetime friends, and their loyalty to others is a key element in their character. They are attractive and animated personalities.

However, Dogs are anxious, terrified of rejection, and insecure about their own talents. Egotism is not a part of their emotional make-up, and the self-effacing Dog has difficulty promoting itself. Securing strong external motivation is important for the Dog, who needs to be urged on by trusted supporters.

Essential Temperament

The Dog's temperament causes them to be very dependent upon their environment. Dog-year people tend to be melancholy and discontent. It is therefore critically important for them to select their environment and associates wisely. Dogs are advised to seek positive, stimulating people who are sympathetic to their feelings, reassuring, and highly affectionate.

There are many variations among Dogs, but one propensity that all share is anxiety. Dogs worry about many things. Most of what they do is motivated by worry. There are shy, reclusive Dogs who devote themselves largely to cultivating inner purity, and there are more high-spirited pups who turn their energies outward to investigate the world. The Dog is a "keen and penetrating observer." Brimming with life, Dogs do more than seek the excitement of new experiences; they are interested in understanding the significance of things and promoting social awareness.

Given encouragement and inspiration, Dogs will bloom and become entertaining companions who are clever and exuberant. With emotional support, the crusading Dog may literally "take on the world," or, at the very least, the neighborhood bully! Those born into Dog years are known for defending those weaker than themselves.

The Other Side—the Dog's Duality

In contrast to their many admirable attributes, unenlightened Dogs can be agitated, secretive, and suspicious. Dogs don't merely take people as they find them, and they can be condescending and moralizing. A Dog's confidence in dealing with other people doesn't carry over into their private lives, and they can be prone to obsessive, dysfunctional relationships with troubled partners.

Caustic words and paranoid behavior represents the Dog's energy being directed in its most unproductive form. Expressed in its darkest form, this energy becomes anxiety, agitation, pessimism, introversion, guarded behavior, criticism, stubbornness, indecision, depression, moralizing, and dependent behavior. The choice lies entirely with the individual. Taken to extreme, masochistic, or anxiety-based personality disorders may develop.

Gifts and Capabilities

The Dog prefers socializing with one or two close friends. Large social gatherings with unfamiliar people and surroundings make a Dog nervous and uncomfortable. One of the reasons for this uneasiness is their basic mistrust of strangers. This idealistic soul searches for worthy causes and is outraged by cruelty and injustice.

A Dog is acutely aware of faults and flaws in others. This natural radar can cause them to become cynical and jump to conclusions, second-guessing to avoid disaster or abandonment. When a Dog enters this "jump to conclusions" mode, they can overinterpret a loved one's words or actions.

Sharp and antagonistic with someone they despise, a Dog will not tolerate anyone who is greedy for power or money, phony, or disloyal. Always the first to speak out against injustice, the Dog's sharp tongue and caustic remarks can shock and cut to the quick. However, Dogs are pugnacious only when diplomacy has failed.

Dogs have a tendency to ask themselves, "What is my purpose in life?" They are acutely aware of their own weaknesses, and frequently mock themselves with self-effacing humor. No one person could ever be as hard on them as a Dog is on itself.

The Dog is devastated by criticism and suffers from deep feelings of self-doubt. This can keep them from taking the first step into uncharted waters. The Dog's brand of anxiety runs deep, and their skin can be thin when chastised.

This animal sign attempts to provide moral support to others, and excels in creating a motivational atmosphere. They are content to work behind the scenes and take up the crosses of others. A distinguishing trait of this sign is a lack of ambition for personal gain, especially financially speaking. When it comes to possessions and portions in life, a Dog will "give away the store." One cannot find a more eloquent, sincere advocate for others.

The Child

As a baby and young child, little Dogs are known to be part of the "syrup of ipecac crowd." Dog children lead the pack in emergency room visits for ingestion of foreign matter other than food products. Pica, as it is called, is prevalent in Dog-year children. Dog children have a hypersensitive sense of smell. Much to their mother's horror, Dog children seem to sniff out medicines, paper products, even bugs and spiders, along with a whole assortment of other quite unappealing odors.

On a social level, Dog children add weekly to their entourage, particularly attracting the small, the picked on, and the friendless.

Dog children often talk early and tend to be quite precocious. They may even seem like little adults at times. This "Jiminy Cricket" of the kindergarten sits on the world's shoulder as a conscience and watchman.

Home and Hearth

Loving parents should go out of their way to give a little extra encouragement to Dog children, as they tend to be more pessimistic and filled with greater anxiety than other children. While these children are active and friendly, they need a great deal of affection and hand-holding. Parents of Dog children can expect to pull their offspring out of many a scuffle and battle, as these little humanitarians stick up for every outcast in the neighborhood.

Favorite escape places for the Dog are romantic landscapes in remote lands alive with legends. Peaceful places by the fireside, far from the aggravating crowds, are also favorite locations.

The most favorable time of year for the Dog is between mid-November and mid-December, when life and creatures enter a state of dormancy and calm.

Auspicious Careers

As a career choice, the Dog can find happiness as a reformer, a teacher, a religious leader, a judge, or a behind-the-scenes advisor. Law, nursing, missionary, and social work strongly appeal to them. As critics, writers, poets, philosophers, and moralists, the Dog finds motivation. Whatever the career, Dog ideas will be profound and often original, delivered with a passion for expression. Dogs are trusted by their employers, and they are gentle souls who are experts when it comes to calming excited people and creating an encouraging ambiance. It is also said that the Dog will find great success in the field of real estate, especially housing.

The Dog dilemma in all career areas will be balancing ongoing conflicts between self-confidence and self-doubt. The Dog must be able to believe in what they are doing and feel committed to a mission or goal if they are to give the best of themselves. This makes them particularly well suited for humanitarian professions and social work.

The Famous and the Infamous

Some famous Dogs you may recognize include Sharon Stone, Sylvester Stallone, Jamie Lee Curtis, Andre Agassi, Cher, Michael Jackson, Madonna, Elvis Presley, David Bowie, Gary Oldman, Claudia Schiffer, Mariah Carey, Rodney Dangerfield, Missy Elliot, Candice Bergman, Kate Bush, Freddie Mercury, Winnie Mandela, Ralph Nader, Mother Theresa, Winston Churchill, Lenin, Voltaire, Socrates, Debussy, John Wesley, Golda Meir, Itzhak Rabin, Jose Carreras, Jacques Cousteau, Sally Field, Victor Hugo, Charles Manson, O.J. Simpson, George Gershwin, David Niven, Judy Garland, Liza Minelli, the artist formally known as Prince, Norman Mailer, Linda Ronstadt, Shirley MacLaine, Brigitte Bardot, Connie Chung, Donald Sutherland, Prince William, Bill Clinton, and Laura and George W. Bush.

Summary

Anxious Dog, this world can be a tough place for your sensitive self. You become disillusioned as you discover the cruel, insincere, and disloyal sides of humanity. But my fellow Dogs, it is not your sole responsibility to safeguard morality. Let's face it—you're a worrier. This can lead to obsession and depression, which are your greatest threats. Be easy on yourself and stop expecting troubles around every corner. Don't waste your life waiting and watching for a foe that never comes. Confide in a straightforward Tiger, a sympathetic Pig, or an optimistic Monkey, and refuse to carry the world's troubles on your shoulders.

Fear,
My old nemesis,
You appear again to
Manipulate, immobilize,
And pervade my eggshell armor.
Come ahead if you will,
And let us do battle.
I am ready.

The Dog Woman

Penny entered this earthly realm as an experienced soul. Spiritually, she carries the world's hopes, fears, and injustices with her. Attached and involved in everything she does, she takes her role in this life seriously and is outraged by indifference. Being of the "yang" disposition, she prefers to stay active. Keeping busy and immersing herself in the problems of others distracts her from her own numerous anxieties and fears.

Penny's physical and emotional health is resilient, and she rises back from crises like a phoenix. Precocious as a child, she looked much older than her age and was speaking in full sentences by the age of 2. Now that she has reached her early 40s, an amazing reverse-aging process has begun, and she is more beautiful and radiant than when she was younger.

Unfortunately, her weak skeletal system doesn't share this youth and causes her innumerable aches and pains. Joint conditions such as arthritis and lower lumbar back pain are chronic sources of discomfort. Penny is very conscious of protecting her back and fragile joints by not lifting improperly and, thereby, worsening the condition. She avoids rigorous exercise routines and instead practices yoga, isometrics, and Pilates to keep fit. Penny also has very delicate skin, which is susceptible to harsh weather conditions, detergents, chemicals, and even stress.

With age and experience has come greater self-confidence, and it was not until midlife that Penny gained enough belief in herself and in her talents to lose many of her phobias and inhibitions.

Sadly, despite being a beautiful and talented woman, Penny has a low sense of self-worth. Prone to anxiety and frustration, she has frequent insomnia and difficulty turning her thoughts off. Silence is her friend, and a lack of it can make her short-tempered and disagreeable. The mental obsessions that have at times turned to compulsions have thrown her emotionally and financially off balance and caused her numerous hardships. Self-destructive vices such as compulsive gambling, self-medication, and masochistic relationships have been her most difficult obstacles to overcome.

Meditation, relaxation, and plenty of peace and quiet are her solutions to achieving serenity. Self-sacrifice is her lifeblood, and she is seldom happy unless giving her time and energy to care for others or a worthy cause. Her need to assist and to protect humanity stems from the deep feelings of unworthiness that haunt her soul.

The causes she chooses to champion almost always pertain to inequality, unfairness, or taking up the gauntlet for the bullied or downtrodden. Penny has been both blessed and cursed with an acute sense of justice and fair play. Her conscious is rarely at peace unless she has done everything in her power to help. This is a soul who has a hyper-vigilant sense of responsibility, loyalty, and dependability. Her sense of obligation, duty, and "doing what needs to be done" is embossed on her spiritual fabric.

Similar to Penny, Beth's anxiety and disappointments are also her worst foes. An idealistic realist, she believes in the innate goodness of the soul, and yet is fully aware of the dark side of the human personality. Beth needs to be needed. She is unselfish with her time and generous with her finances. Being a woman who naturally forms strong bonds with others, apathy or indifference cuts her deeply. Rejection and abandonment are almost unbearable for her.

It has also been difficult for Beth to break off difficult relationships. Her profound loyalty can indeed backfire when she is unable to "detach." Indeed, it is almost impossible for Beth to take a more detached position, even if her emotional or physical health may be suffering. Ingratitude from others is part and parcel to her over-generosity, which may or may not be well received. Unfortunately, some people are suspicious of random acts of kindness.

A curious irony is that, despite having such earnest affection for her loved ones, Beth is uncomfortable expressing these feelings. Once again, her subconscious sense of inadequacy restrains her. This serious and reserved soul needs to play and romp like the puppy that abides within her.

Normally friendly and effusive, when her ingrained anxiety rears its ugly head, Beth's mood turns dark. She hurls harsh and moralizing comments, and others are well advised to retreat until her alarm has subsided. Pessimism, panic, and being judgmental are some of her least admirable character traits. They occur when Beth is feeling a sense of "powerlessness" over her life.

Motivated, reliable, and conscientious, both Penny and Beth share the anxiety and watchfulness that their Dog year has bestowed upon them. Each need a strong external source of encouragement and emotional support. Both women approach life with great caution and apprehension, both are fearful of rejection, and neither can live without tenderness and affection.

The Dog Man

Eddie has perfected the art of looking busy and worried, and he is a man of humanitarian principles and deep convictions.

Eddie still lives in the small mountain town where he was raised, and his roots in the community run deep. He returned to his hometown after graduating from college with a degree in Land Management. Following a successful career in real estate, he decided to run for public office (and won).

Despite the sacrifices involved, Eddie always fights for what he believes in, and is the first person to step forward as an advocate for the people of his small county. Unfair property taxes, shortages in social services, and corrupt spending practices are just some of the issues this urban vigilante has waged war upon.

A passionate advocate of human dignity, Eddie is not content to watch the world go by. From early childhood, he has stood up to bullies both big and small. Eddie makes sure that others don't forget the rules of playing fair or that there is a *new* sheriff in town.

While Eddie is blessed with many fine qualities, he tends to unwittingly antagonize people with his outspoken moral scrutiny. When he feels that his ethics or principles are on the line, no power on Earth can silence him, and his ordinary humility goes right out the door.

Eddie gives a lot and asks little in return. But his spirit is desperately in need of reassurance, kindness, and love. Cold shoulders and apathy cut him to the core, and others would seldom guess how vulnerable he is. It would be most beneficial for him to acquire some detachment and a thicker emotional skin.

His stamina and endurance have grown stronger as he has aged, but his joints may tend to stiffen with advancing age. Staying physically active will preserve his energy and flexibility. However, convincing Eddie to see a doctor for a checkup is a formidable task. His motto is "no news is good news," and he doesn't see the need to go to the physician if he can "get there on his own two feet."

Eddie exercises considerable self-control over his emotions, despite their intensity. If betrayed or dishonored, his revenge is tempered with exceptional patience and usually served cold.

Always a rebel at heart, William is actually more humane than radical. The revolutions he participates in have to do with compassion and high ideals rather than anarchy. Blessed with a fine soul, William is honest and despises hypocrites. He would never sell out, despite the consequences.

Confidant to friends and family alike, William's modest manner and self-effacing ways make him approachable, and others readily confide in him. Never one to flaunt himself, William prefers to stay behind the scenes and keep a low profile. Compliments tend to embarrass him, and he rarely seeks to promote himself. Underneath his somber appearance lies a generous, tender, and loving soul. His devotion to those in his inner circle is unparalleled.

However, despite his exceptional virtues, William is not an easy man to live with. His moods tend to fluctuate between childlike optimism and fatalism with predictable regularity. At these "prophet of doom" times, William will retreat, becoming uncommunicative and brooding. High-minded plans turn into pessimistic fears, and his problems take on a catastrophic appearance.

Any woman with serious designs on this man should arm herself with much patience and refrain from forcing him into making a declaration of love, let alone a proposal of marriage. The woman who will win his heart will have proven her loyalty over time.

Eddie and William both possess a profound sense of "decency." Each is shy, unpolished, and has difficulty relaxing and seeing the lighter side of life. Constantly "on guard," these men have a strong "fight or flight" reaction, originating from their constant anxiety. Both tend to see trouble around every corner, and each will worry about many things in their life.

Chapter 14

The Pig/Boar

The Tolerant Pig (Hai)— the "Accommodating Pacifist"

January 30, 1911 to February 17, 1912: Metal Pig
February 16, 1923 to February 4, 1924: Water Pig
February 4, 1935 to January 23, 1936: Wood Pig
January 22, 1947 to February 9, 1948: Fire Pig
February 8, 1959 to January 27, 1960: Earth Pig
January 27, 1971 to January 15, 1972: Metal Pig
February 13, 1983 to February 1, 1984: Water Pig
January 31, 1995 to February 18, 1996: Wood Pig
February 18, 2007 to February 6, 2008: Fire Pig
February 5, 2019 to January 24, 2020: Earth Pig

Polarity: yin (negative)
Sign order: 12th
Alternate name: Boar
Symbolism: zen, yin
 and yang
Lucky colors: black, white
Fragrance: floral
Flavor: spicy, salty

Food/beverage: delicatessen foods, cheeses, dark ale/beer
Flower: chrysanthemum
Gem: topaz
Feng shui direction: north-northwest
Lucky number: five

The 12th and last position in the Chinese Zodiac, the Pig, is a gentle-hearted and long-suffering sign. Those souls born into Pig years learn the lesson of "resignation"—they have the ability to accept others, and understand that human nature is controlled by fate and that a higher power is at work. The Pig is a wise but passive observer rather than an active participant throughout life. Pigs are highly intelligent, and possess an unique sense of dry humor. However, rarely will they apply their intelligence to gain dominance.

Gentle yet strong of will, those who are born under the sign of the Pig are tolerant, sincere, and honest. Known to be studious and well informed, the Pig chooses few friends, remaining loyal for life. Through the good times, and especially the bad times, you can always count on a Pig to be there. Pigs relish long-standing relationships and are affectionate and openhearted.

Peaceful Pigs recoil from confrontations and have difficulty saying no. The rapidly acquiescing Pig forgives easily and takes blame unduly.

The most favorable time of day for those born into Pig years is between the hours of 9 p.m. and 11 p.m., when the yin force intensifies in strength and families settle in for a sound night of slumber. As the cycle of the day draws to a close, the Pig contemplates the day's happenings and blissfully dozes off, listening to the quiet voice of their heart.

Essential Temperament

The Pig hates hypocrisy, phoniness, lying, and all forms of unkindness. These souls love the comforts of life, especially adequate affection. If these souls have an Achilles' heel, it would have to be a weakness for the sensual pleasures of life.

Here we find a jewel of an individual, stable, mature, and long-suffering to a fault. Possessing intelligence, empathy, and meticulous attention to detail, in every way the Pig is a "keeper."

Pig-year souls have a strong need to set difficult goals and see them through. The perfect home for a Pig person is a country house with a view of the mountains on one side, and the ocean on the other, blissfully shared with their beloved. Pig souls wish to surround themselves with beauty, liberty, fresh air, and plenty of greenery. Emotional therapy can be found in a walk along the beach or sitting amidst the forest reading the poetry of John Muir.

The Other Side—the Pig's Duality

In contrast to their many admirable attributes, unenlightened Pigs can be passive, self-indulgent, and slothful. The Pig's apparent passivity and ability to take people as they find them is many times used as an excuse to avoid making decisions. The Pig's search for earthly pleasures can also blindside them and lead them down a destructive path to licentiousness and debauchery. Dysfunctional Pigs may deliberately choose difficult or neurotic partners.

Expressed in its darkest form, the Pig's energy becomes extreme naiveté, defenselessness, a lack of competitive spirit, pragmatism, and over reliance on physical or material comforts. The choice lies entirely with the individual. Taken to extreme, panic disorders and obsessive-compulsive tendencies may develop.

Gifts and Capabilities

Those born into a Pig year can respond to disappointment by withdrawing and isolating themselves. Once equilibrium has been restored, however, they return to devote themselves once again to the issue at hand. Pig-year souls are genuinely nice, and the sweetness of their personality is filled with a clever wit. Those who know them are always a bit shocked, yet amused, by their slightly off-color humor.

Pigs prove tolerant companions. They are patient, genuine, and upstanding, but, more often than not, they fail to receive reciprocal treatment from others. Pigs can suffer from gullibility, as they project their own integrity onto others and naturally assume others will respond in a similar fashion. Unfortunately, many people are opportunistic and take advantage of the Pig's trusting heart.

The Chinese believe that if the Pig's birth date is well before the traditional Chinese New Year's feast, the Pig will escape many of the disappointments in life. The closer the birth date is to the lunar New Year, the more likely it is that the Pig will be duped or betrayed.

The early childhood years are usually a time of calmness and security. Many Pig's long to return to such a time. The Pig may not be recognized for their talents and kindness until midlife approaches, but most are compensated generously at this time. During midlife, relationship dilemmas could be a problem, and emotionally injurious self-imposed isolation or solitary suffering could result. Confiding in friends and family may permit the Pig to commiserate, but they prefer to handle conflicts internally.

Once past the struggles of midlife, a Pig's retirement years are generally emotionally satisfying, peaceful, and content.

The Child

The parent lucky enough to have this sweet little bundle is indeed fortunate. Absolutely cuddly and loving, this child is almost too good to be true. Deeply conscience of right and wrong, the Pig child will prefer to passively watch the world from a distance, resigned to the way things are.

Little Pigs like to sleep a lot, and enjoy good food. Chivalrous even as small children, the sick parent or relative of a Pig child will have many handmade get-well cards, tucked covers, and much touching concern. Here are the Boy and Girl Scouts of the Eastern Zodiac.

Pure of heart, Pig children can tend to be gullible, and parents need to make sure that these children don't give more than they take with friends. Meticulous with possessions and life in general, children born into Pig years tend to be hypersensitive during childhood, but they will be compensated by being financially fortunate later in life.

Home and Hearth

The Pig is the paragon of parental devotion. Consumed with protective instincts, they find great happiness in devoting themselves to the welfare of their children. Pig parents are more comfortable acting as a friend to their little ones. They have difficulty being strict disciplinarians. They handle children wisely and lovingly. Despite being well-mannered and a peace-loving, Pigs can become ferocious boars and frenzied sows when it comes to defending their children.

The most favorable time of year for Pigs is between mid-December and mid-January, at the end of the lunar–solar year, when everyone is busily preparing for the feasts and celebrations of the New Year holiday.

Auspicious Careers

According to Chinese legend, the peace-loving Pig is the luckiest sign in business. They often make their mark in the arts, or as entertainers, but also make splendid researchers, scientists, and computer programmers. Pigs may also prosper as filmmakers, writers, poets, painters, and entrepreneurs. Educators, attorneys, and physicians are also often found amongst Pig natives. Though never willing to employ underhanded methods, these souls are usually successful at earning money. Through thick and thin, a Pig will hang on in business and ride out tough times. They are often rewarded for this financially.

The Famous and the Infamous

Some famous as well as infamous Pigs include Winona Ryder, Stephen King, Val Kilmer, Minnie Driver, Noah Wyle, Christina Applegate, Jada Pinkett-Smith, Billy Crystal, Tom Arnold, Edward James Olmos, Emma Thompson, Arnold Schwarzenegger, Hillary Rodham Clinton, Woody Allen, Julie Andrews, Richard Dreyfuss, Sheena Easton, Farrah Fawcett, Marie Osmond, Carlos Santana, Brian May, Tracey Ullman, Phil Donahue, Luciano Pavarotti, Nastassja Kinski, Randy Travis, Rosanna Arquette, Elton John, Steven Spielberg, Ernest Hemingway, Humphrey Bogart, Lucille Ball, Ginger Rogers, Fred Astaire, Henry Kissinger, Oliver Cromwell, Samuel F. Morse, Noel Coward, Edgar Rice Burroughs, Ralph Waldo Emerson, Carl G. Jung, Henry Ford, and the Dalai Lama.

Summary

Proper Pig, we love you for your virtue, your kindness, and for your tolerance with fools. If we would just take your advice and walk the straight and narrow, we wouldn't get into so many tight squeezes. But your penchant toward prudence can make some of us feel like naughty children. A weak person is liable to be bullied; a tamed horse is often ridden. This proverb warns that weakness is a disadvantage. When confronting those with evil intent, you must be firm or risk being pushed around. Be the same kind of friend to yourself as you are to others. Bless you!

Life is so fragile,
Like a shadow on water
Broken by the wind.

The Pig Woman

Jen is perhaps the most sincere and honest woman one will ever meet. Compassionate, forgiving, and truthful, she is a conscientious wife and loyal friend. She is exceedingly frank, yet speaks with the sincere conviction of a child. She lives in the country and loves long walks in the quiet forest. Her home is well separated from her neighbors so as to provide her with necessary peace and privacy.

While Jen is a charming and remarkable woman, her gentle and accommodating personality often seems too good to be true and tends to be taken for granted by others. But true it is, and it is without a trace of hostility or aggression. This "saint" of the Chinese Zodiac is self-effacing, sympathetic, and deeply affectionate.

At age 25, Jen still lives with her parents, and is in no hurry to flee the nest. Her respect and reverence for her elders is just one of the many sterling character traits she possesses.

Jen admits that she looks for a husband who has the same virtues as her father. These are some tall shoes to fill. Her perfect partner must be mature, protective, and decisive. Her strong attachments to her family and to the past make her sentimental to a fault. Revering the past, she associates it with security and the carefree time of her youth. She has a certain innocence about her, and a touching frailty that makes others want to shield her from life's arrows.

This personification of womanhood is fearful of suffering, unpleasant surprises, and personal criticism. Jen is a marvelous hostess, and her home is always neat and tidy. She is seldom happier than when at home with her children and pets.

Financial security is also essential to her emotional stability, but she tends to be inconsistent in her spending habits (she either spends too freely or pinches her pennies). Unbridled ambition is a foreign concept to Jen, but Chinese tradition says that she will always be lucky financially and that she will be blessed with abundance and wealth in her old age.

Sarah's idea of happiness is a cozy home filled with rosy-cheeked cherubs and a chivalrous husband who buffers her from harsh reality. Her feminine rhythms are strongly connected to the lunar cycles, and her extremely emotional nature ebbs and flows throughout the month.

She differs from her Pig-year brothers in that she has no hesitation in seeking a medical opinion regarding various woes. Her physical health is so tightly intertwined with her emotional health that they are almost one in the same. A personal crisis can provoke all manner of physical symptoms for her, and psychosomatic illnesses of mysterious origin have occurred during the times when she felt unable to cope. Her lunar hormonal fluctuations also account for her vacillation between serenity and distress, and calmness and fear.

Sarah tends to be gullible, impressionable, and highly sensitive to suggestion. It is important to her psychological balance that she not accommodate so frequently, and stand up for her own interests more often.

Self-inflicted "heart wrenching" is her specialty, and she can't help but dwell in the past and what she "should have done." She is deeply romantic and extravagantly emotional. At the moment, Sarah has her mother living with her, which has put a strain on her marriage (she can sometimes be a victim of her own kindness).

Both Jen and Sarah are gentle and impressionable souls. They need solitude, peppered with moments of passion. Home-loving, loyal, and earthy, each can be stubborn and obstinate, and both often hesitate to take the initiative. Always the support persons and seemingly timid, there abides within a tenacious, persevering, and patient soul.

The Pig Man

Kevin is the personification of a "yin" male. Sensitive, vulnerable, and noble, his reflective, nurturing night-force is immediately recognizable. A loner and an eccentric, Kevin was a father at an early age. What his children lack in discipline they make up for in sentimentality and creativity.

This lovable man possesses rare traits of chivalry and old-fashioned values of days gone by. Distressed, for example, by the sight of a homeless, suffering animal by the side of the road, he keeps a healthy distance from the harsh realities of life.

Rarely indulging in competition, especially at the expense of another, people feel at ease in his presence. His essence of "resignation" accepts others at face value, and he will never seek to proselytize or convert another to his way of thinking. However, his sincerity inspires confidence in his pragmatic conclusions.

Kevin is a poet at heart, and he is blessed with both creativity and a vivid imagination. He has chosen to channel this into the world of computer programming and considers himself an artist who "paints with 1's and 0's." His computer software programs are both reliable and aesthetic. Kevin's inquisitive mind and multifaceted intelligence also has the boost of a sixth sense, his intuition being impeccable.

Kevin is slow to anger and tolerant with those he loves. He can be trusted not to lose his head or act irrationally, even under the most trying circumstances. Merciful with children and pets alike, his limitless compassion is long-suffering (even with the foolish).

His health is fairly resilient, but he suffers from a delicate digestive system. Stress, disrupted relationships, and lack of sleep can send his nervous system into an electrical storm, and Kevin must be careful not to combine stress and insomnia. He should also keep a healthy distance from life-dramas, which can leave him emotionally exhausted.

Mild mannered and rarely aggressive, Kevin can be overly apologetic. His modest and low-key spirit hates quarreling and any form of argument. Aggressive competition repulses him, and he is not a fan of football, boxing, or other violent contact sports. He would much rather spend a Saturday evening simply enjoying life, sipping fine wine, and watching the sun set, hand-in-hand with his wife. Simplicity is his recipe for happiness.

Like Kevin, Nguyen does not make friends easily, nor does he readily let others into his inner circle. While admittedly very human,

Nguyen's unfavorable character traits are practically nonexistent when compared to his more esteemed qualities.

In true British form, Nguyen is tight-lipped and stoic. He is too shy to ask for help and too private to let others be privy to his problems. Outwardly relaxed and carefree, he keeps tightly hidden his fixation on the dark and tragic aspects of life, and his sentimental musings upon days gone by keep him ever attached to his family.

Although his faults are few, they do exist. Nguyen is essentially passive. He is generally unwilling to force a confrontation or fight unless absolutely necessary. Sometimes this results in his compromising when it would serve him best to stand his ground. Also, his noncompetitive nature holds him back from receiving the recognition due him.

Financially, he is prudent and would never gamble away his life savings at the casino tables. Ironically, he is often "spontaneously lucky" with money. He is the one who must be coerced into putting even a nickel into a slot machine—and then hits the jackpot.

Love is always serious business to both Kevin and Nguyen. Vulnerable and capable of complete devotion, they are not one-night-stand lovers. Possessing an enormous capacity for love, each is a tender, kind, and demonstrative partner. Always ready to oblige, both of these men are genuinely good human beings (lovers, rather than fighters). They prefer to please and their hearts are forever tried and true.

Chapter 15

The Elements

The Heavenly Stems With the Earthly Branches

While each sign of the Chinese Zodiac repeats every 12 years, the specific combination of animal sign (Earthly Branch) and element (Heavenly Stem) occur only once every 60 years.

In addition to the 12 animal signs, traditional Chinese astrology or "Chinese chance," as it is sometimes called, is modified or flavored in a different way by each of the five basic elements. Wood, Fire, Earth, Metal, and Water constitute these five elements, or "courses." The interrelationships between these basic elements constitute a fundamental principle in Asian philosophy. A well-balanced mix of each element in one's birth chart and environment is desirable.

There exist two natural, complementary (yet contradictory) forces in our universe—the yin and yang. The yin (negative) represents the female, dark, soft, moist, nighttime, and docile aspects of life; the yang (positive) represents the male, positive, bright, hard, dry, daytime, and dominant aspects of life. The yin and the yang are continually in a state of movement and change, and are always seeking "balance." When one moves, the other responds.

Our universe consists of five basic elements. These elements are Wood (growth), Fire (leadership), Earth (stability), Metal (structure), and Water (feelings). Everything, including humans, in the universe between heaven and Earth has a relationship with these five elements. These five essential elements apply to all physical phenomena, including colors, directions, seasons, and sounds. They also apply to the years, months, days, and hours of the Chinese calendar.

The Doctrine of the Five Elements

The doctrine of the Five Elements consists of two fundamental principles. The first principle is that each of the five elements produce, enable, support, and assist one another. The second principle is that each of the elements destroy, control, destabilize, and fight one another.

Wood produces Fire.

Fire creates Earth.

Earth supports Metal.

Metal compliments Water.

Water assists Wood.

Fire destroys Metal.

Metal is hostile to Wood.

Wood fights Earth.

Earth conflicts with Water.

Water extinguishes Fire.

The entire universe is composed of these five elements. They are in an interconnected balance with one another.

The Creative Cycles

The five elements have both a creative cycle and a destructive cycle. The creative cycle is one of positive movement and creative change. The creative cycle begins with Wood feeding the Fire. When the Fire is burned up, what is left is ash, or Earth. From the Earth, Metal is created, such as gold. Metal attracts Water by way of condensation. The Water then feeds the wood, allowing it to grow.

The Destructive Cycles

The destructive cycle is one of negative movement and resistance to change. Water puts out Fire, and Fire destroys Metal through heating action (metal loses its form). Metal destroys Wood (like a saw cutting through it). Wood depletes Earth by absorbing its nutrients. Earth destroys Water by turning it into mud.

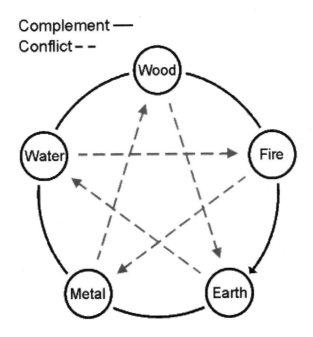

The Yin Conductive, Producing, Supporting Forces

The productive relationships support, help, and produce things within the universe.

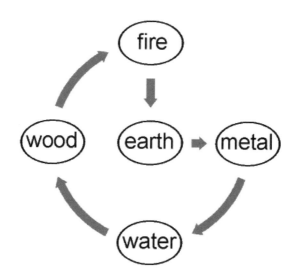

By means of Metal emerges Water—Metal transforms into liquid if heated. Metal can hold Water. Metal is the supporting element of Water. Water can release the power of Metal.

By means of Water comes Wood—Water brings vegetation, which grows into Wood. Water helps trees (Wood) grow. Water is the supporting element of Wood. Wood can release the power of Water.

By means of Wood comes Fire—Fire is built and sustained by burning Wood fuel. Wood helps Fire to burn. Wood is the supporting element of Fire. Fire can release the power of Wood.

By means of Fire comes Earth—Fire breaks down its fuel which returns to the Earth. Fire helps produce dust (Earth). Fire is the supporting element of Earth. Earth can release the power of Fire.

By means of Earth comes Metal—Metal and precious gems origi-
nate within the Earth. Earth helps minerals (Metal) to form. Earth is
the supporting element of Metal. Metal can release the power of Earth.

The Yang Inhibiting, Controlling, Destroying Forces

These hostility relationships bring fighting, conflict, and destabilize the universe.

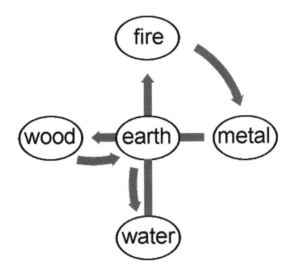

Each element has a relationship with all of the others. These relationships between the elements are noted by following the arrows on
the graphic.

Metal is destroyed by Fire when melted by heat. Fire can melt
Metal, but Metal might not melt before Fire is extinguished. Fire and
Metal are enemies. Fire overwhelms the movement of Metal.

Fire is destroyed when extinguished by Water. Water can extinguish Fire, but Fire might evaporate Water. Water and Fire are enemies. Water overwhelms the movement of Fire.

Water is destroyed and controlled by Earth when it is absorbed, and its path is channeled or trapped. Earth can absorb Water, but Water can cover the land (Earth). Earth and Water are enemies. Earth overwhelms the movement of Water.

Earth is destroyed and controlled by Wood when nutrients are extracted, yet plant life keeps Earth from eroding. Wood can break the ground (Earth), but Earth buries and traps Wood. Wood and Earth are enemies. Wood overwhelms the movement of Earth.

Wood is destroyed and reduced by sharpened Metal tools. Metal can cut Wood, but Metal might become dull before breaking Wood. Metal and Wood are enemies. Metal overwhelms the movement of Wood.

These five elements are constantly moving, waning, waxing, and changing. In Eastern philosophy, the soul is said to move through large cycles of 60-year periods. This large cycle consists of five smaller cycles represented by each of the five elements.

Wood represents the first 12 years of life—the period of rapid growth, symbolized by trees, plants, and vegetation.

Fire represents the second 12 years of life—the leadership and the idealism of adolescence, symbolized by fire, heat, and light.

Earth represents the third 12-year period of life—the stability of early adulthood, symbolized by soil and the Earth itself.

Metal represents the next "fixed" and solid period of middle age. This period is symbolized by minerals, gold, jewelry, iron, rock, and hard surfaces.

Water: represents the reflective and wise fifth twelve year periodthis period is symbolized by liquids, cold, and soft surfaces.

At age 60, the 12-year cycles begin anew, returning to the Wood stage (representing new growth, regeneration, and "second" childhood).

It is during this period that one begins anew on their journey through the astrological element sign combinations.

Wood

The Wood element represents the period from birth to age 12—a time of rapid mental and physical development, imagination, creativity, simplicity, and compassion.

Likened to a great sequoia, the nature of Wood is to move upward toward the light, to spread outward, and to expand. Its "middle-of-the-road" nature is devoted to goodwill, the arts, aesthetic pursuits, and to beauty. Wood-element people have high-minded values and believe in the dignity of every human being. Those born into the Wood element understand the value of teamwork and excel in organizing extensive and complex projects.

The Wood element expands, and brings cooperation and persuasion. Wood-element people are progressive in their thinking and futuristic in their goals and ventures. The Wood element endows each sign with a natural presence and sense of propriety; however, Wood can also incinerate, and often encompasses a combustible temper. The Wood element represents idealism, imagination, the family, and artistic theory.

The element of Wood relates to the physical organs of the liver and gallbladder. The flavor associated with this element is acidic, with beneficial foods consisting of wheat and poultry. The color of Wood is green. Wood corresponds to the morning, the season of spring, and to the wind. The feng shui direction assigned to the Wood element is east, representing family, stability, and the tall, slender, cylindrical shapes of columns or a tower.

Wood is most compatible with Fire, Earth, or Water elements. Some effort is needed when interacting with other Wood-element people, and there is potential for serious conflict and misunderstandings between yourself and those born under the Metal element.

Wood-Element Combinations

The Wood Rat is diligent, successful, and is blessed with a curious and inquisitive mind. A youthful, forward-moving Rat, who loves to find out how things work. This is a social and friendly soul, but the Wood Rat may have trouble with intimacy and experience a tumultuous love life. Agreeable and thoughtful of others, they seek acknowledgment and approval. Wood Rats seek security and will always plan for their future.

The Wood Ox possesses authority and a natural presence. Their relentless determination assures them of success in life. This is the most artistic of the Oxen, and is oftentimes blessed with profound mechanical aptitude. Music, creative writing, and poetry all come naturally to the Wood Ox. A natural leader and authority, this soul may encounter rivalries and jealousies from less-talented individuals.

The Wood Tiger is a more sedate personality. They are not as impetuous as other Tigers and prefer to look before they leap. Impartial and a good judge of character, they are intellectual and understand the importance of team effort. Wood Tigers will have diverse friends, some from unusual or eccentric lifestyles. Group efforts bring them great popularity. The Wood Tiger changes professions frequently, as this Tiger outgrows positions, moving ever upward.

The Wood Rabbit possesses poetic gifts and is attracted to the fine arts. Gardening and landscaping will please their sense of beauty and harmony while fulfilling their need for space and freedom. The Wood Rabbit is an outwardly shy, highly intuitive, and deep-feeling soul. This is the gentle seducer who shuns and avoids restraints and obligations. Wood Rabbits are collectors of art, antiques, and other objects of beauty.

The Wood Dragon is imaginative and talented, and is able to improvise when faced with chaotic or unexpected events. This Dragon possesses the gift of creative invention and is attracted to nature and symbols of beauty. The Wood Dragon has a dual nature; they are dynamic and courageous, yet seductive and seeking to please.

This is a practical Dragon, whose feet are firmly planted on the ground. This is also a more moderate Dragon, less prone to have a heated temper.

The Wood Snake craves quiet, stability, and plenty of privacy. This is a sympathetic and earnest Snake, who shares their philosophical ideas with all who care to listen. This Snake has a strong need for independence and can successfully take on large projects. The aesthetic nature of Wood blesses this Snake with a love of culture and the fine arts. Wood Snakes are possessive and very protective of their home and family.

The Wood Horse has a quick and disciplined mind, is cheerful, cooperative, and is a team player. Changes and new innovations capture their vivid imaginations. They are also progressive and modern thinkers. The Wood Horse is the most social of all the Horse–element combinations. They are amusing, good conversationalists, and are attracted to theater, public speaking, as well as to sports and athletics.

The Wood Goat tends to worry more than other Goats. They are romantic, acquiescing, generous, and well-liked. This is a courteous Goat with a good sense of humor. The Wood Goats are the most sentimental of the Goat–element combinations, and are eager to please those whom they love. This is a nurturing Goat who has a soft heart toward stray animals and compassion for friends down on their luck. The Wood Goat always gives freely of their resources.

The Wood Monkey is resourceful and enthusiastic, but may have trouble slowing down or pacing themselves. This Monkey maintains high standards for themselves, as well as for others. They are gregarious, socially adept, and possesses a quick-witted sense of humor. Personal expression is essential to the Wood Monkey, and they are active participants in life. Their curious minds excel at solving difficult problems, and they are never without resources.

The Wood Rooster is more thoughtful and tactful than other Rooster–element combinations. They are open-minded, ambitious, and happiest amongst a social group, sharing lively conversation. Wood Roosters are also passionate, and just as Wood can incinerate, they are susceptible to excesses at times. They must use their clear-sightedness to avoid getting carried away or pushed to excessive anger. The Wood Rooster gains equilibrium and self-assurance closer to midlife.

The Wood Dog is affectionate, youthful, and known for its strong convictions. This is the "team player" of the Dog–element combinations. Idealistic and eager to learn, the Wood Dog is popular and forms intimate bonds with others. This is a charming, personable soul who defends their values with tenacity and tact. Watchful and nurturing, Wood Dogs can organize major projects and manage large groups of people with ease.

The Wood Pig is a well-balanced and charming soul who loves to be close to nature, the woods, and the earth. The Wood element plays the role of "muse" for this Pig, who may very well express itself through the arts. Possessing uncanny intuition and influence, the Wood Pig is passionate, bawdy, and cannot live without physical love. The Wood element may also urge this Pig to commit excesses with both food and drink.

Fire

The Fire element represents the period from ages 13 to 24—the adolescent time of dynamic passion, energy, aggression, and leadership.

The nature of Fire is to consume, to resolve, and to bring about an outcome. The Fire element will multiply each sign's inborn talents and energies. Fire-element people have the gifts of leadership, passion, and assertiveness. Those born into the Fire element rarely have trouble making decisions, as they are decisive and masterful. They attract others with their strong and radiant personalities.

The Fire element arouses, changes, and converts. Fire-element souls have an abundance of energy that may cause the individual to be impatient when pursuing goals. The movement of Fire is rapid and can consume one's energies if not balanced with relaxation and moderation.

The Fire element represents the ability to be decisive, to lead, and to act spontaneously without forethought. This element punctuates each sign with an exclamation mark.

The element of Fire relates to the physical organ of the heart, blood, and the circulatory system. The flavor associated with this element is bitter, and meals of rice and lamb are beneficial. The color designated to Fire is red, and fire corresponds to the noon hour and the hot season of summer. The feng shui direction assigned to the Fire element is south, and is represented by pointed, sharp edges and angular mountain peaks.

The elements that share the greatest compatibility with Fire are Wood, Earth, and Metal. Extra effort is needed in relationships with other Fire-element people, and there is potential for serious conflict and misunderstandings between them and those born into the Water element.

Fire-Element Combinations

The Fire Rat is determined and self-disciplined. They are enthusiastic regarding their projects and must guard against overwork. This is a soul of strong moral principles and high-minded thinking. This perpetual, eternal student absorbs knowledge like a sponge and is well versed in a wide variety of subjects. The Fire Rat loves travel and fashionable clothes, and is more aggressive by nature than other Rat–element combinations. The Fire Rat is the most generous of the Rats and is capable of leadership.

The Fire Ox is talented with their hands and highly creative. The Fire Ox has tremendous energy, and this can make them impatient to reach their goals. This Ox must be cautious not to reach a level of exhaustion and to respect their body's limits. The Fire Ox is a conqueror and may be drawn to politics, or perhaps even the military; however, they will always remain fiercely individualistic. The Fire Ox is family-oriented, and is always king or queen of their castle.

The Fire Tiger has been blessed with extraordinary leadership aptitude. Fire Tigers are volatile and passionate in life and in love.

The Fire Tiger may find it hard to delay gratification, and patience isn't their strong point. Always up for a new adventure, the Fire Tiger is action-oriented, extravagant, and expressive! Rather nomadic by nature, Fire Tigers enjoy frequent changes of environment and are rarely content staying anywhere for too long. These are the most independent members of the Tiger's pride.

The Fire Rabbit is more high-spirited and stubborn than other Rabbit–element combinations. They personify the Rabbit essence of "detachment." Fire Rabbits will have a tendency to keep their distance, especially when feeling rejected or excluded. The Fire element releases a boldness that will overcome the Rabbit's natural reticence. More outspoken than other Rabbit–element combinations, the Fire Rabbit has an inner flame that strengthens their courage and adds aggression to their personality.

The Fire Dragon is more ambitious than other Dragon–element combinations. They are articulate in speech and have a tremendous desire to succeed. They are hard workers, natural thespians, and born leaders. Fire Dragons are admired for their integrity and forthright manner. This Dragon is the most strong-willed of the Dragons, and they tend to rely on their own judgment without taking into account other's views. Humility is difficult for the Fire Dragon, and admiration is what they seek.

The Fire Snake is decisive and more self-assured than other Snake–element combinations. They are healthy and vital, ambitious, confident, natural leaders, and tough enough to get the job done. The Fire Snake tends to be more forceful, outgoing, and energetic than some of the other Snakes, but remains compassionate and deep-thinking. This Snake wins respect and support with their firm and persistent manner. They possess an excellent sense of humor and have a wide circle of friends.

The Fire Horse will make their mark early in life and exhibit their various talents in astonishing ways. The soul born under this influence will be endowed with superior wisdom, but perseverence may be difficult. Fire Horses display above-average qualities of leadership and draw others to their warmth and brilliance. Both the positive and negative characteristics of the Fire Horse will be multiplied tenfold, as this is the most ardent and impetuous of Horse–element combinations.

The Fire Goat is a strong personality. Blessed with extraordinary artistic talents, the Goat is a natural writer, poet, and artisan. The Fire Goat is more expressive than other Goat–element combinations. Generous and charismatic, this Goat inspires others and is one of the only Goats aggressive enough to be a leader. They are extroverted and charming, but they can also be self-indulgent and manipulative.

The Fire Monkey is competitive and popular. Having wide and diverse interests, this energetic and animated Monkey is a problem-solver and a self-starter. Fire Monkeys are creative, resourceful, and highly competitive. The Fire element imparts great vitality and good health, but could also consume much of their energy. Their fertile imagination produces an ingenious albeit suspicious personality.

The Fire Rooster is intense, energetic, and a natural leader. This lively Rooster has difficulty staying on one subject and can have many projects in the works. The Fire Rooster is self-assured and determined, and also expressive and brutally candid with their observations. The Fire element imparts great vitality and a highly competitive nature. Mercurial, zealous, and suspicious of other's motives, this is the most strong-willed of the Rooster–element combinations.

The Fire Dog is dynamic and connects easily with others. They are opinionated, dynamic, and radiant with energy. Highly animated and outspoken, Fire Dogs have no problem expressing themselves, and many choose to go into politics or the entertainment industry. The Fire Dog has an alluring and friendly personality that conceals a self-effacing and anxious Spirit. Possessing great charm, the Fire Dog stands their ground and is fierce only when diplomacy has failed, but fierce nonetheless.

The Fire Pig is decisive and more self-assured than other Pig–element combinations. This is an alluring soul, opinionated, adventuresome, and radiant with energy. The Fire Pig is most fortunate financially due to their combination of ambition and purity of heart. Fire bestows leadership abilities and bravery to this soul, and the Fire Pig often chooses to be a "first-responder" by profession. Many are firemen, police officers, and emergency workers.

Earth

The Earth element represents the period of life from ages 25 to 36—the young adult period characterized by stability, reliability, practicality, industry, and common sense.

The nature of Earth is to stabilize, to keep whole, and to preserve. The Earth element is symbolic of the mother's protective womb of peace and safety. Those born under the Earth element are both practical and intuitive. They have exceptional powers of organization and are competent masterminds and executives.

Stability, practicality, and reliability characterize those influenced by the Earth element. Its natives are capable of making wise and sensible decisions. Those born under this element's influence are honest, serious, and tend to be conservative. The Earth element represents patience, whether it be with a hyperactive 2 year old or with a difficult spouse. Earth element natives are firmly anchored, family-oriented, and live in the moment.

The element of Earth relates to the physical organs of the spleen and the stomach. The flavor associated with this element is sweetness, and the most beneficial foods are corn and beef. The colors designated to Earth are yellow and brown and this element corresponds to the afternoon, the periods between seasons, and humidity. The feng shui direction assigned to the Earth element is the center, or middle, representing practicality. The Earth element is symbolized by squares and boxed shapes.

Earth signs greatest compatibility is with the Metal, Fire, and Water elements. Earth-element natives must work harder in relationships with other Earth-element people, and serious conflict and misunderstanding can arise between yourself and those born under the Wood element.

Earth-Element Combinations

The Earth Rat is sensible and alert. They have remarkable willpower, but they also have a tendency to worry about security and finances. The Earth element tempers the high-strung Rat personality and provides a nurturing, down-to-earth temperament. The Earth element makes this Rat prudent, crafty, and subtle. Earth Rats need activity to keep them from dwelling on (and thus, becoming mired in) their own problems.

The Earth Ox is the most loyal and steadfast of the Oxen family. Stoic on the outside, yet vulnerable on the inside, the Earth Ox is a deep thinker and tends to be a loner. Food and the Earth itself serve as refuges that entices the Earth Ox to close the door on the human race and pursue meditation, relaxation, and solitude. Enduring and persistent, this is the slowest (but surest) of all the Oxen.

The Earth Tiger looks for practicality in everything they undertake. The Earth Tiger is not as hotheaded as other Tigers, and possesses a more mature temperament. The Earth Tiger is deeply conscientious and humanitarian in spirit. A fair-minded leader, the Earth Tiger makes an excellent counselor, mentor, or judge.

The Earth Rabbit has excellent deductive powers and prefers solid and reliable pursuits. The Earth element endows them with more foresight and capacity for organization. This is the most conservative of the Rabbit–element combinations. The Earth Rabbit is wise and sensible with financial matters. They are also quiet, critical, serious, introverted, and respected. This is the consummate diplomat and peacemaker.

The Earth Dragon is more realistic than other Dragons, but does enjoy accumulating wealth and speculating on the future. A conscientious and hard worker, the Earth Dragon takes on chores and problems that others find impossible to conquer. Prudent, yet suspicious, the Earth

Dragon has eyes in the back of its head and misses nothing. This is the most nurturing soul of the Dragon family; they are always willing to help out in a crisis, and they are fiercely protective of family and loved ones.

The Earth Snake is a secure and cozy Snake who loves elegance and the material comforts in life. With an ability to turn inward and retreat from the outside world, the Earth Snake is relaxed and, at times, even lethargic. They are the most prone to "hibernation," and many choose a reclusive life of spirituality and contemplation. This is a dreamy, stay-at-home Snake who is often sought out for their wise counsel.

The Earth Horse is careful, capable, and sensible. Those Horses born under this influence are methodical in manner, excellent managers, and reinforce solid foundations in all that they do. Conservative by nature, the Earth Horse is a realist and one who knows how to advance prudently and skeptically. This is a less-ambitious, yet more meticulous, Horse; with a tendency to be possessive, they are often very security conscious.

The Earth Goat is sympathetic, honest, and well liked. Financially fortunate, the Earth Goat has a taste for luxury and the finer things in life. The Earth Goat is the most suspicious and mistrustful Goat-element combination. They exhibit unpredictable moods and mental processes. The Earth Goat isn't as outgoing as the other Goats, and their friendships must stand the test of time. This is the most artistic and deep-thinking soul of the Goat family; one who lives in a world of dreams and fantasy.

The Earth Monkey is well informed, benevolent, and kind. They can be cursed with perfectionist ways and are more pragmatic and realistic than other Monkeys. Most of their enterprises are motivated by a need to expand and a desire for increasing possessions. This Monkey likes activities that will bear fruit and is attracted to speculation, sales, and real estate. The Earth Monkey can be fearful about the future; still, they have been blessed with financial intuition and good monetary instincts.

The Earth Rooster has a profound perspective on life and is the most persistent and persevering of the Rooster–element combinations. This Rooster does not like to take risks and has the ability to build upon the previous work of others. Success, security, and appearance are important elements in the life of the Earth Rooster. They will bury their treasures safely away. Earth Roosters are realistic, pragmatic, and shrewd.

The Earth Dog possesses a powerful need for recognition and appreciation. They are capable of devoting themselves totally to a cause or to achieving social ambitions. The Earth Dog is long-suffering in love, and is both independent and gifted. However, they can be taken advantage of due to their overly generous nature. The Earth Dog jealously protects their home and loved ones, is extremely proud, and can always be counted on to be a fair and impartial mediator.

The Earth Pig is shrewd and imaginative, but perfectly realistic and materialistic. Earth Pigs are strong and self-confident, and they enjoy socializing with their inner circle of trusted friends. This is an artistic Pig, who may express its artistry via practical and pragmatic avenues, such as computers and logic systems. This combination of sign and element creates a soul who appears to be submissive, but in fact, is in control from behind the scenes.

Metal

The Metal element represents the period from the ages of 36 to 48—the middle age of life characterized by fixed values, strength of will, and fluency of speech.

The nature of Metal is to define and strengthen. The Metal element symbolizes clear thinking, sincerity, and accuracy. Metal-element people have the gift of "structure," and the ability to interface with the outside world. Those born into the Metal element set and follow their goals with fervor and passion. Metal is determined and fixed, holding each sign in a position of strength by serving as a foundation and base.

The Metal element will also add rigidity to a sign. This firm element is without movement and can contribute to stubbornness and reluctance to compromise. Metal-element people speak candidly and bluntly, as the Metal element represents strength of will and fluency of speech. Those souls born into Metal-element years are fiercely independent, solitary, and blessed with perseverance.

The element of Metal relates to the physical organs of the lungs and the large intestine. The flavor associated with this element is pungency, and beneficial foods include oats and meat. The color designated to Metal is white, and it corresponds to night, the season of autumn, and dryness. The feng shui direction assigned to the Metal element is west (representing creativity), and this element is symbolized by the curved shape of rounded hills or a dome.

Metal is most compatiable with Wood, Earth, and Water elements. Extra effort is needed when dealing with other Metal-element people; similarly, serious conflicts and misunderstandings can arise between this element and those born under the Fire element.

Metal-Element Combinations

The Metal Rat is extremely emotional, a shrewd socialite, and knows how to use the system to get ahead. The Metal Rat can be rigid and adamant in expressing their opinions. Argumentative when provoked, this Rat has a sharp tongue and is capable of verbally tattering an opponent. This Rat is very success-oriented, with strong monetary instincts and the ability to save for a rainy day.

The Metal Ox can be rigid and, at times, even severe. Metal Oxen are ambitious, success-oriented, and unwavering in determination. This strong combination of sign and element is steeped in duty and is not easily swayed (even by hardships, drawbacks, or initial failures). The Metal Ox is financially fortunate, constant, and true to their word, and they can make an articulate moral arbitrator or judge.

The Metal Tiger is glamorous and distinctive in appearance. This Tiger has much ambition and is fascinating to those around them. Although their goals may change from time to time, the Metal element bestows perseverance to the Tiger. Metal Tigers will be unbending and daring in expression. For greatest success, the Metal Tiger must be able to compromise with those who are in a position to benefit them.

The Metal Rabbit is clever and sly; they also are often endowed with much artistic ability, and a deeply romantic core. This is a "solitary" element, which intensifies the need for privacy and is manifested in a lonewolf-style of problem solving. This Rabbit likes to mix in the best circles and usually has an intimate, but very loyal, group of friends. This is the most private of the Rabbits; they are not prone to compromise and are a soul who keeps their own counsel.

The Metal Dragon is capable and cunning, and particularly shrewd in business matters; this is due to the Metal element contributing to its good financial sense. Metal Dragons are the most sharp-tongued of the Dragon family, can be argumentative, and are natural-born leaders. They are attracted to spiritual pursuits and tend to isolate themselves for periods of solitary contemplation. This is an energetic and decisive Dragon who excels at commanding others and facing confrontation.

The Metal Snake is cautious and skeptical. They keep their own counsel and prefer to work independently. They are capable of great profit and wealth, as strong financial instincts are present with this combination of sign and element. The Metal Snake is also blessed with acute intelligence and a deeply sensitive core. These souls have a tremendous ability to influence the outcome of situations. They are quiet, confident, and have a cultured appreciation of the fine arts, literature, and music.

The Metal Horse has a magnetic personality, is undeterred when it comes to career ambitions, and is the dynamic cutting blade of the Horse family. Effective and an expert in their area of interest, the Metal Horse does not hesitate to act quickly on a decision and will readily take on a crusade or worthy cause. Just and honest, this Horse is an ardent idealist, humanitarian in nature, and has very high standards for both themselves and others.

The Metal Goat has the heart of a warrior beneath their easygoing exterior. These souls are not as harmless as they look, and are more energetic and decisive than the other Goat–element combinations. The Earth Goat is a perfectionist and has a tendency to judge. They are a curious mixture of compromise and stubbornness, and dependence and self-sufficency, and oftentimes seem contradictory. The influence of Metal on the Goat is light and easy in some situations, yet rigid and uncompromising in others.

The Metal Monkey is independent and astute. While they are determined souls, they can also become frustrated by failure and can be impatient with their life progress. Metal Monkeys tend to be more rigid in their beliefs, are attracted to metaphysics, and are not as social as other Monkeys. The Metal Monkey will strive for high social positions and are experts in implementing plans. They are usually involved with the nuts and bolts of putting an idea together.

The Metal Rooster is analytical and a hard worker. Compromise may be difficult for them, and they may feel unappreciated at times. Nothing could be farther from the truth, as Metal Roosters are indispensable to their family, friends, and employers. Metal Roosters are the most opinionated and oratory types of Roosters. Powerfully candid, the Metal Rooster has a gift for captivating an audience with their shrewd and brilliant powers of deduction.

The Metal Dog is not as influenced by external circumstances as the other Dog–element combinations, and this independent thinker follows their own path. If there is a flaw in someone or something, the Metal Dog will spot it. Metal Dogs are very success-oriented and steady in their determination. These Dogs are not as encumbered by the usual Dog anxiety, but their principles of loyalty and honesty remain quite rigid. The Metal Dog will vacillate between a desire for material success and an equally strong desire for spiritual reflection. They are more serious than other Dogs and remain idealistic-realists.

The Metal Pig likes the sure and predictable in life and will scrutinize everything with their most analytical eye. The Metal Pig is the most rigid of the Pig–element combinations and can, at times, throw away a good situation because it does not conform to expectations. Metal Pigs are ambitious and clear-sighted, and thus often enjoy success. They possesses a warm and more outgoing nature than other Pig–element combinations and usually enjoy a larger circle of friends than other Pigs.

Water

The Water element represents the last and final period in the 60-year cycle between the ages of 48 to 60, and this stage is characterized by the powers of reflection, sensitivity, and persuasiveness.

The nature of Water is that of feelings and emotions. Water descends, seeks out, and fills low places, especially the hearts of the disheartened and needy. Those born into the Water element are guided by their feelings and the need to communicate. The Water element endows one with a lucid and quick mind; however, this element is chaotic because it does not have its own form and tends to take on the shape of whatever contains it.

Water-element people possess the ability to persuade others and manipulate their environment. The Water element also brings the gift of empathy and bestows a more sedate nature to each sign. Water-element natives view life objectively and are much sought after for their counsel. The Water element blesses its natives with a deep spiritual nature and the ability to thrive in social contexts. Those born into Water years possess extraordinary intuition and often function as a kind of spiritual barometer in this life.

The element of Water relates to the physical organs of the kidneys and bladder. The flavor associated with this element is saltiness, and beneficial foods are peas and pork. The color designated to Water is black or dark blue, and this element corresponds to the midnight hours, the season of winter, and coldness. The feng shui direction assigned to the Water element is north, representing flowing emotions and wavy lines and shapes.

Water signs are most compatible with those born under the elements of Metal, Wood, and Fire. Water must make an extra effort when dealing with other Water-element people; similarly, serious conflicts and misunderstandings can arise between Water people and those born into Earth-element years.

Water-Element Combinations

The Water Rat is an open-minded Rat, and they are always looking for new ideas and experiences. This is a very sensitive soul who empathizes with others. With their fine vocabulary and vivid imagination, Water Rats excel in language, writing, and journalism. This Rat knows how to communicate, and they can easily influence the populous. The Water element produces a soul who is deeply emotional and more introverted than other Rats.

The Water Ox has a knack for accurately gauging future potentials and for utilizing the talents and resources of others. The Water Ox will be able to wear away at even the toughest rock in life with silent, yet constant, efforts. This intuitive Ox prefers to infiltrate, rather than dominate as other Oxen-element combinations do. They have a way with words and a talent that causes others to want what they want; thus they can achieve their goals in an indirect way.

The Water Tiger is a humanitarian and empathetic soul, and has a more serene and sedate nature than other Tigers. These are the dreamers and the artists of the Tiger kingdom. Their manner is less brusque and their edges are not as rough as other Tiger–element combinations. They have been blessed with a judicious insight into human nature and have a sixth sense. The Water Tiger is exquisitely sensitive, and many pursue positions of spiritual leadership.

The Water Rabbit is sensitive and well liked. Their sensitive feelings can be soothed with plenty of tender, loving care and liberal doses of the finer things in life. The Water element intensifies the sensitivity of this Rabbit–element combination. The Water Rabbit is a deep thinker and possesses enhanced intuition, bordering on psychic. They are admired for their good taste and are highly valued for their advice.

The Water Dragon is extremely gifted and has a more sedate nature than other Dragon–element combinations. This is a liberal-minded Dragon, always open to new ideas and experiences. They have a true gift for seeing things objectively and creating a foundation in all that they do. The Water Dragon is humane, an excellent judge of the truth, and they excel in any type of public relations work or public speaking.

The Water Snake is charismatic, capable, and blessed with an insightful and intuitive radar. They have a well-developed ability to communicate with others. They are empathetic and have a multitude of interests. Water Snakes have a gift for seeing things objectively, and this combination of sign and element is a compassionate and excellent judge of human character. Because of this, Water Snakes are often highly sought after as advisors and financiers.

The Water Horse advances their own ideas through their convincing speech, thereby influencing the thoughts of others. This is an open-minded Horse, always seeking new ideas and experiences. They have a gift for seeing things objectively, and are viewed as humorous and friendly. The Water Horse is able to convey their emotions powerfully, and has an insatiable need for movement and decisive action.

The Water Goat is the most sensual of the Goat family and possesses remarkable street smarts. They do need much emotional support however, and loyalty is of supreme importance to the Water Goat. Poets abound amongst the Water Goats, and many talented writers, artists, and performers are found with this combination of sign and element. The Water Goat is the most peace-loving of Goats, and is determinedly humanitarian.

The Water Monkey is tolerant and thoughtful. More inclined to moderation than other Monkey–element combinations, they rarely take themselves too seriously and are full of humor and good cheer. The Water Monkey has a deep need to communicate with others. They cannot tolerate boredom, routine, or the stagnation of their keen mind. Water Monkeys possess a stealthy nature and further their cause by influencing and persuading others.

The Water Rooster is energetic and possesses an enjoyable sense of humor. They do, however, have a tendency to worry excessively at times. This is the intellectual type of Rooster who will enjoy cultural pursuits. With Water as this Rooster's element, they will be given to clear thinking and compassion. The Water Rooster is proficient in the use of the written word and is a commanding speaker capable of swaying other's opinions.

The Water Dog is talented and intuitive. They can be very persuasive for the right cause, and others see them as kind and compassionate. Water is an exceptionally empathetic influence on the already tenderhearted Dog, and this makes the Dog capable of great sacrifice. Always scrupulous and virtuous, the Water Dog's principal quality is loyalty. Occasionally lacking self-confidence, this emotional Dog needs much encouragement from others to assuage their self-doubts.

The Water Pig is shy and quiet, yet able to articulately express themselves. They are hardworking and loyal, but may have felt restrained at early periods in life. Competition does not interest them in the least, and what they seek is peace and tranquillity. This most private of the Pig family is intuitive to the point of clairvoyance. They prefer to live within a safe and comfortable world of love and affection.

	ELEMENTS				
	Wood	**Fire**	**Earth**	**Metal**	**Water**
Color	Green	Red	Yellow/ Brown	White	Black/Blue
Season	Spring	Summer	Between Seasons	Fall	Winter
Direction	East	South	Center	West	North
Foods	Sour	Bitter	Sweet	Spicy	Salty
Fruit	Palm	Almond	Date	Peach	Chestnut
Organs	Liver	Heart	Spleen	Lungs	Kidneys
System	Nervous	Circulatory	Digestive	Respiratory	Excretory
Face	Eyes	Tongue	Mouth	Nose	Ears
Emotion	Anger	Happy	Worry	Sad	Fear
Weather	Windy	Hot	Wet	Dry	Cold
Personal	Honest	Polite	Loyal	Famous	Gentle

Chapter 16

Your Birth Time Companion

By this chapter, you may have recognized your own traits, as well as the traits of others symbolized by the 12 astrological signs and the 12 combinations of elements. The 12 animal symbols used to predict and explain the characteristics of each year are also used to predict and explain the influence of the day and nighttime hours in which you were born. Each animal sign influences a two-hour period of a 24-hour day. One's companion hour also modifies and "shades" the personality. This is your "other self" that reveals hidden spiritual possibilities. It is your shadow self and advisor in life. Locate your birth hour and see how it influences your sign.

11PM - 1AM	Rat 鼠	子	Tze
1AM - 3AM	Ox 牛	丑	Chou
3AM - 5AM	Tiger 虎	寅	Yin
5AM - 7AM	Rabbit 兔	卯	Mao
7AM - 9AM	Dragon 龍	辰	Chen
9AM - 11AM	Snake 蛇	巳	Si
11AM - 1PM	Horse 馬	午	Wu
1PM - 3PM	Goat 羊	未	Wei
3PM - 5PM	Monkey 猴	申	Shen
5PM - 7PM	Rooster 雞	酉	You
7PM - 9PM	Dog 狗	戌	Xu
9PM - 11PM	Pig 豬	亥	Hai

The Hour of the Rat

The charming and intelligent Rat rules those born during the midnight hours of 11 p.m. to 1 a.m. You will be more outgoing, sociable, and cautious with money. The essence of the Rat is "concealment." This indicates an extra cautious and eclectic personality, with the classic Rat traits such as writing talent, acute intelligence, hyper-sexuality, and social charm accentuated. Especially favorable companions to the Rat are the Rabbit, Horse, Monkey, and Pig.

The Hour of the Ox

Those born during the hours of the solitary and serious Ox, 1 a.m. to 3 a.m., are influenced by a restrained, cautious, and steady influence. The essence of the Ox is that of endurance. Hardworking and strong -willed, the Ox is a natural authority and powerful speaker. This companion promotes self-confidence, willpower, and authority. Especially good combinations with the Ox are the Tiger, Goat, and Rabbit (for balance).

The Hour of the Tiger

The adventurous Tiger rules signs born during the dark predawn hours between 3 a.m. and 5 a.m. This companion is a dynamic and stirring influence that influences your birth sign to be more outgoing, more action-oriented, and more impulsive. The essence of the Tiger is that of nobility. The Tiger intends to win at life, and can have a self-assured, almost majestic influence on an individual. Tiger hours influence all signs to be more self-reliant, more adventurous, and more passionate. Good advisors for the Tiger are the Horse, Ox, Snake, and native Tigers.

The Hour of the Rabbit

The well-mannered Rabbit rules signs born between 5 a.m. and 7 a.m., just as the sun is rising. The personality of someone born during this time will be more moderate, reflective, diplomatic, and discreet. The well-mannered Rabbit has strong artistic instincts and may influence the individual to collect art and antiques. The essence of the Rabbit personality is detachment. Those born during Rabbit hours require more privacy, tranquility, and peacefulness. Favorable companions for the Rabbit are the Dragon, Rat, Rooster, and Monkey.

The Hour of the Dragon

The powerful Dragon rules signs born during the energetic morning hours of 7 a.m. and 9 a.m. This birth sign has extra strength, determination, and added ambition. The essence of the Dragon is that of unpredictability. The Dragon has strong opinions, and is very outspoken. They possesses great luck, exceptional health, and dramatic energy. The autonomous Dragon is a good companion for the Monkey, Goat, Cat, and Dog.

The Hour of the Snake

The wise and philosophical Snake rules the routine mid-morning hours between 9 a.m. and 11 a.m. Those born during Snake hours are more intuitive, reflective, and private. With this stealth and mystic companion, birth signs receive behind-the-scenes influence and are armed with the patience to wait for the right time to make their mark. The essence of the Snake is a quiet, gathered strength. With the Snake as companion, an individual sign becomes more wise, cultivated, cerebral, seductive, accommodating, intuitive, attractive, reflective, organized, alert, sympathetic, elegant, soft-spoken, compassionate, and calm. Harmonious pairings are the Goat, Pig, Tiger, and Dog.

The Hour of the Horse

The physically active Horse rules those born between the hours of 11 a.m. and 1 p.m. This birth hour imparts a high activity level and the need to be in perpetual motion. The essence of the Horse is decisiveness. The Horse is a gifted orator and public speaker, extremely self-confident, and attracted by all that shines. With the Horse as a companion in life, a birth sign will need an exciting path that always looks toward the future. This companion influences a sign to be more adventurous, daring, and future-oriented. Favorable combinations for the hour of the Horse are the Dog, Pig, Rabbit, and Snake.

The Hour of the Goat

The whimsical and artistic Goat rules the early afternoon hours between 1 p.m. and 3 p.m. The spirit and substance of the Goat is propriety, and the sweet-natured Goat as companion will influence a birth sign to be more tolerant, easy-going, and receptive. The Goat lends a dreamy and artistic influence in an ensemble of capricious mental clouds. Imagination, a love of fantasy, and creative elegance characterize those born into Goat hours. The delicate and kind Goat resists schedules, as well as adds the yin—the negative feminine force to a personality. Auspicious companions are the Snake, Ox, Rooster, and Dragon.

The Hour of the Monkey

The mischievous and fun-loving Monkey rules signs born in the late afternoon hours between 3 p.m. and 5 p.m. The Monkey's charm and shrewd (though jovial) nature contribute mental agility and profound powers of persuasion. The Monkey will usually have a card up their sleeve and embody irrepressibility. This companion imparts a delicious sense of humor to each sign it is coupled with. The Monkey can sell just about anything to anyone, and provides an aptitude for entrepreneurial enterprises. The Monkey, as a companion, imparts wit, enthusiasm, and eternal youthfulness to a sign and can serve as a beneficial guide to the Ox, Rat, Goat, and Snake.

The Hour of the Rooster

The methodical Rooster rules those signs born between the rejuvenating early evening hours of 5 p.m. and 7 p.m. The core of the Rooster soul is "application," and symbolizes the ability to defer gratification in order to enjoy the future rewards. The flamboyant and extroverted Rooster will increase a sign's efficiency and contribute a lively and outgoing manner. Roosters are concerned with appearance and love pageantry. The Rooster as companion will nudge the individual to be impeccably dressed and verbally candid, and separate mundane activities from future goals. The Rooster is a good companion for the Tiger, Ox, Rabbit, and Horse.

The Hour of the Dog

The watchful and wary Dog rules those born between the relaxing middle evening hours of 7 p.m. and 9 p.m. Your sign will take on the guardian nature of the Dog (a watchful, dutiful, and loyal influence, that can be anxious at times). This companion contributes a bit of the pessimistic Dog outlook on life and is capable of great sacrifice for the right cause. The Dog's magnanimous nature influences your sign to be nonmaterialistic, reasonable, and fair-minded. The Dog quickly assesses any situation and takes up the gauntlet for others. The Hour of the Dog is a lucky companion for the Tiger, Goat, and Dragon.

The Hour of the Pig

The obliging and truthful Pig rules signs born between the sleepy hours of 9 p.m. and 11 p.m. Those born during Pig hours will be more peaceful, reclusive, and sensitive; however, they are also sociable, content, and self-indulgent. This is a solitary yet caring companion, and one that motivates altruism. The Pig companion contributes a touch of vulnerability and naivety. It also motivates one to acquire fine treasures and worldly goods. This is a favorable birth hour for the Rat, Dragon, and Monkey.

Chapter 17

Chinese Love Signs— Karmic Connections

Eastern sages have known for millenniums that certain souls seek each other out. Powerfully drawn together by what some people call "chemistry," or "that certain something," specific signs act as magnets to one another. These unusual attractions are sometimes unexplainable. Some examples of these "karmic connections" include a strikingly handsome man happily married to a simple, somewhat physically unattractive woman; a brilliant and well-educated woman happily betrothed to an uncomplicated man with little formal education; a wealthy person quite happily in love with someone from poverty-stricken roots.

From these examples, and countless others, it is evident that physical appearance, professional aspirations, and social circumstances are not responsible for the surprising attraction that exists between certain souls. This attraction is not based on sexuality alone. These deep and unseen connections underlie close family members, best friends, special bonds with specific pets, as well as love and sexual relationships. They are "spiritual rendezvous," if you will, between kindred and familiar souls.

Thousands of years of experience have borne out some rather striking consistencies of attraction. While relationships are possible between all signs, some combinations are inherently happier and more harmonious than others.

Compatibility and Attraction

Why do these instant attractions exist? What is behind the urge to be close to one person and not another? What motivates people to throw all caution to the wind to seek out a relationship with another so unsuited for them? Perhaps you've even asked these questions about your own relationships. Chinese astrology proposes a paradigm of relationships between signs that explains this phenomenon.

In the Triangles of Compatibility graph, you will notice that the 12 signs are arranged together in four groupings of three. These notable compatibility groupings are known for their affection and like-mindedness. These four complimentary trinities walk hand in hand through the realm of the heart.

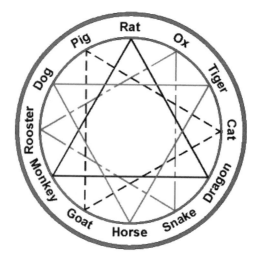

First Compatibility Trine

The achievement-oriented and visionary signs of the Rat, Dragon, and Monkey comprise the first compatible trinity. They are intense and enthusiastic lovers. In life and in love, these three tend toward restlessness and intend to accomplish what they set out to do. Impetuous and easily frustrated, these three soul mates are irrepressible, unpredictable, and possess potent positive yang energy.

Second Compatibility Trine

The conservative and consistent signs of the Ox, Snake, and Rooster comprise the second harmonious trinity. These three soul mates conquer life through endurance, application, and the slow accumulation of energy. Although each sign is fixed and rigid in opinions and views, they are geniuses in the art of meticulous planning and understand the wisdom of deferred gratification. Each one is a stable and long-lasting love partner ruled by deep, dark negative yin energy.

Third Compatibility Trine

The public-spirited souls of the Tiger, Horse, and the Dog comprise the third compatibility group. These three signs seek one another's company and are like-minded in their pursuit of humanitarian causes. Each excels in verbal communication and is a gifted orator. Relationships and personal connections are their highest priority and each one seeks their intimate soul mate in this life. Idealistic, decisive, and noble, these three signs are passionate and earthy lovers ruled by the aggressive positive yang energy.

Fourth Compatibility Trine

The peaceful and empathetic signs of the Rabbit, Goat, and Pig complete each other in their quest for the aesthetic and beautiful in this life. These three signs are artistic, refined, and well-mannered. They desire the preliminaries in romance and are the fine artists of lovemaking. Possessing more placid temperaments than the other nine signs, each one recoils and detaches from strife and ugliness.

Their reflective negative yin energy seeks an aesthetic, yet dominant, yang positive lover.

Incompatibility and Oppositions

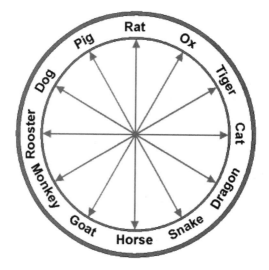

Sometimes two souls meet and seem to clash immediately. There is incompatibility between signs in direct opposition to each other. This dynamic explains an interaction with a person who is so kind to others, yet rather brusque with you. When interacting with a polarized opposite, you may encounter antagonism; lack of cooperation; and tense, unhappy unions. While fascinated by, and initially attracted to each other, those signs in direct opposition will eventually repel each other due to clashes in essential disposition.

For instance, the stealthy demeanor and occasional elastic conscience of the Snake will frustrate and antagonize the honest and forthright Pig. In kind, the carefree, easy manner of the Horse could incite the nervous Rat to emotional tantrum level. The self-assured Dragon may never relate to the Dog's exasperatingly self-effacing ways, and so on.

Of interesting note concerning the oppositions: each is said to "open the money vault" for one another. Oppositional signs can be most auspicious in business, bringing to the table what the other lacks.

Signs in direct opposition include:

The Rat and the Horse

The Ox and the Goat

The Tiger and the Monkey

The Rabbit and the Rooster

The Dragon and the Dog

The Snake and the Pig

Soul Mates and Combatants

Shown in the following Soul Mates/Combatants below are some arcane relationships rarely spoken of that are neither placed within the trines of compatibility nor in opposition to each other. These extreme combinations of signs are the "soul mates" of each sign and in drastic reverse—the karmic "combatants" of each sign. While the soul mates often celebrate golden wedding anniversaries, in contrast, there are also two signs that are locked in unseen combat with one another.

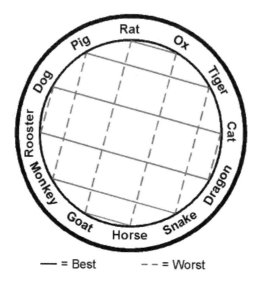

— = Best   - - - = Worst

In the graph, notice that outside of the compatibility triangles and oppositions there are the best and worst pairings for each of the 12 signs. While the Goat, Rabbit, and Pig are the best of friends, it is with the extroverted Horse that the Goat will find their soul mate. Rat souls are highly compatible with both the Dragon and the Monkey, but it is with the stoic Ox that the Rat will find their soul mate.

Soul Mates

The Rat and the Ox
The Tiger and the Pig
The Rabbit and the Dog
The Dragon and the Rooster
The Snake and the Monkey
The Horse and the Goat

Similar in extreme energies, while the Dog and Dragon experience friction due to their direct opposition, it is with the critical Rooster that the Dog will find their greatest challenge. The Tiger and the Monkey will never see eye-to-eye, but it is with the languishing Snake that the Tiger will experience the greatest frustration, and even tangible animosity.

Karmic Combatants

The Rat and the Goat
The Ox and the Horse
The Tiger and the Snake
The Rabbit and the Dragon
The Monkey and the Pig
The Dog and the Rooster

Relationship Rainbow

Signs that are not in opposition, not within the triangles of compatibility, and not considered soul mate/combatants will be compatible in various colorful degrees.

	Rat	Ox	Tiger	Rabbit	Dragon	Snake	Horse	Goat	Monkey	Rooster	Dog	Pig
Rat	A-	A+	C	D	A-	D	D	F	A-	C-	C	B
Ox	A+	C	B	B	C	A-	F	D	D	A-	C	C
Tiger	C	B	D	C	B	F	A-	C	D	B	A-	A+
Rabbit	D	B	C	A-	D	A-	C	A-	B	D	A+	A-
Dragon	A-	C	B	D	A-	C	B	C	A-	A+	D	B
Snake	D	A-	F	A-	C	B	C	C	A+	A-	B	D
Horse	D	F	A-	C	B	C	A-	A+	C	B	A-	B
Goat	F	D	C	A-	C	C	A+	A-	B	C	D	A-
Monkey	A-	C	D	B	A-	A+	C	B	A-	B	B	F
Rooster	C-	A-	B	D	A+	A-	B	C	B	D	F	C
Dog	C	C	A-	A+	D	B	A-	D	B	F	B	B
Pig	B	C	A+	A-	B	D	B	A-	F	C	B	A-

Key:

A+	Outstanding! A soulmate.
A-	Excellent. Good marrige.
B	Very good. Different enough to be fun.
C	Fair–Moderate. Some tolerance needed.
F	Very bad. Difficulty and strong conflicts.

The Rat and Love

It is after sunset, during the midnight hours they rule, that Rats come alive with numerous acquaintances, lively discussion, and intensely romantic interludes. The Rat soul values companionship and love more than anything else. Rats are ardent lovers and exuberantly express the physical aspect of their love. However, despite an abundance of eclectic charm, they often suffer from loneliness. Rats tend to have legions of acquaintances, but very few close friends. This deeply emotional soul yearns for affection and sincere attention. To love and to be understood is as vital to this sign as breathing. Rats need a partner to cherish as well as one who cherishes them in return.

Romantically, the best match for the Rat is with the Dragon or Monkey; however, their true soul mate is the Ox. Rats should be particularly cautious in love relationships with a Goat or Horse.

Rat—Rat

These two like-minded souls will seek to achieve a complete merging of body and spirit. Both are imaginative lovers who refuse to settle down in routine. However, both being yang positive souls, it is important for each to take the lead in romance. Each partner's high-strung disposition may exacerbate worries, affecting productivity.

Rat—Ox

So sentimental and vulnerable is the Rat to their soul mate, the Ox, that this tender soul may sacrifice their finances at love's altar. There can be nothing too good or too costly for their beloved Ox. With this potent combination, the Rat's usual perceptive discernment and shrewd financial sense can go right out the window.

Rat—Tiger

This unlikely match is a common one that "looks good on paper," but may fail to provide emotional satisfaction to both parties. The Tiger overshadows their Rat partner just by being themselves and always being on the go. This leaves their Rat partner feeling abandoned and inadequate.

Rat—Rabbit

The Rat soul cannot live without communication, and the detached Rabbit can leave the Rat feeling empty and abandoned. The Rabbit is not as invested in the relationship as is their Rat partner and will often become the artful dodger.

Rat—Dragon

When married, even in the face of a dalliance, emotional security reins supreme with these two souls; if a choice must be made between a spouse and a lover, there is no contest. Both of these souls recognize each other's taste for variety.

Rat—Snake

When it comes to lovemaking, the Rat is a master and virtuoso, and sex is something they are capable of surrendering themselves to, body and soul. This highly interests the Snake, but the Snake's taste for forbidden fruit could devastate the hypersensitive Rat's sense of home and hearth (and Rats will rarely forgive the infidelity).

Rat—Horse

Despite their opposition, these two souls interestingly enough hook up with each other frequently. However, a dichotomy exists within Rats between a need for security and a need for independence. They need an understanding ear to listen to their ideas, and the Horse is too preoccupied with their own dreams and ambitions. This is a relationship that can end in bitterness.

Rat—Goat

This relationship is a comedy of errors. By the time the leisurely Goat wakes up to face the world, the energetic Rat has almost completed their day. Hyperactivity meets sloth, and the results can be inharmonious, to say the least.

Rat—Monkey

Sexuality is an art and fine science between Rats and Monkeys. These two love each other and are not bashful about showing it. They may have many exhausting nights of love intertwined with intellectual conversations and confidences.

Rat—Rooster

Rats do not enjoy being left alone with no one to speak to, and they need to exchange ideas (cementing their own positions in the process). This works well with the equally interactive Rooster, but the Rat is too sensitive to withstand the Rooster's caustic criticisms.

Rat—Dog

The Rat can't help correcting the Dog's all too human errors, and the Dog feels belittled and not up to par—a disaster from an insecure Dog's point of view. The relationship resembles that of a parent/child relationship, which leads to power struggles and difficult interactions. Any infidelity on the Rat's part will be considered absolute treason.

Rat—Pig

Rats have a tendency to feel as if nobody understands them. Feeling understood in a love relationship is important for their peace of mind, and the compassionate Pig fits the emotional bill nicely. (But then who doesn't get along with the Pig?)

The Ox and Love

Never make the mistake of assuming those souls born into Ox years are dispassionate or unromantic. This is a fallacy that stems from their unwillingness to indulge in trite romantic displays to express their love. They prove their love in sensible ways. Being realists rather than romantics, sentiment tends to be closely connected with duty to the responsible Ox. In romance, the Ox's slow, patient, and consistent character may attract the opposite sort: those who vacillate and are less secure. Oxen are vulnerable in love. They are persevering, yet slightly naïve, and their trust must be given to one who will never break faith with them. However, although deeply partner-oriented, Oxen can live quite well independently. Oxen are easy-going and good-natured as both friends and lovers.

The most auspicious soul mate and romantic match for the Ox is the intellectual and home-loving Rat. The Ox and the Rat can form relationships of long duration. Both the Rooster and the Snake are also excellent choices for enduring relationships. Partnerships with the capricious Goat or the pontificating Horse may be challenging.

Ox—Rat

These two signs form a mutual admiration society and compliment each other well. Both souls are family- and security-oriented and work together well in life and in love. When beside this "right partner," the Ox will remain devoted for life.

Ox—Ox

These two strong personalities can form a happy, quiet couple. It is important that both see eye-to-eye on key life issues, such as religion and politics, to avoid a clash of wills. Both are placid, home loving, and hardworking—a recipe for success.

Ox—Tiger

Here we find "two cooks in the kitchen," and these two natural leaders may vie for pole position in their relationship. Each party must have respect for their agreed-upon areas of authority.

Ox—Rabbit

These two are both "very yin" and solitary loners by nature. The Rabbit will expect the Ox to take the lead in this relationship, regardless of the gender of each partner. The Oxen's brand of love is stable and practical, while the Rabbit needs luxury and pampering.

Ox—Dragon

A clash of wills could derail the course of any long-term relationship between these two. Well-defined roles and mutual respect is critical between them in order for a warm and enduring union to form.

Ox—Snake

This combination is exemplified by a cozy fireside relationship between these two karmic best friends. Each has a deep understanding of one another. There is excellent compatibility in friendship and in marriage for these two like-minded souls.

Ox—Horse

The Horse would rather be anyplace but home. This is nothing less than treason to the Ox, who holds the family circle in such reverence. The Horse interprets the Ox's stability as boredom, and neither sign has the foggiest idea of how the other thinks or feels.

Ox—Goat

This is a case of the motorcycle cop with a quota to meet and the low-key small-town sheriff who wants no confrontation. Oxen are regulated, organized, and controlled. Goats are loose cannons that capriciously act and react to life. This is not an auspicious combination.

Ox—Monkey

Because of their self-sufficient and practical nature, love and sex are important, though not absolutely essential to Oxen. This throws a wet blanket on the Monkey's enthusiasm, thereby creating a difficult relationship.

Ox—Rooster

The Ox delights in the company of the efficient Rooster. Whether it's a female Ox keeping the home fires burning for her Rooster military husband, or a male Ox enjoying watching his "little firecracker" Rooster wife efficiently run their home, this is a match made to last.

Ox—Dog

This could be a maudlin pity party waiting to happen, and a double-dose of pessimism does neither of these two souls any good. However, the Dog has much compassion for the sweet-natured yet awkward Ox, and this can be a nurturing and loyal relationship.

Ox—Pig

These two calm souls speak the same language of quiet strength and old-fashioned virtues. However, the Ox and Pig do not normally gravitate to each other. Each being quiet and solitary souls, unless introduced by a third party, there romantic sparks might never ignite.

The Tiger and Love

The Tiger's need for passion and new triumphs can produce an adventure movie of a love life. Impetuous and impassioned, Tigers discover their sensuality early in life. These souls are deeply feeling and sentimental, but they must part ways with a relationship that has become boring, unchallenging, or claustrophobic. Tigers have a need to respect their lovers. They possess an independent soul and require much personal space. Tigers need a soul mate that is ready and eager to follow them. Physically restless, the earthy Tiger is protective, territorial, and always in forward motion. Romantically intense and possessive Tigers thrive on risk and are known to seek out challenging mates.

Romantically, the best match for the Tiger is anyone born during Horse or Dog years; however, their true soul mate is found with the honest and obliging Pig. They are wise to be cautious in love relationships with Monkeys, Snakes, and other Tigers.

Tiger—Rat

This union is a frustrating one for couples. The Tiger is forthright, and one always knows where they stand with them. The Rat is concealed and their motives are not always evident. This is a relationship without connection, and one where each person may eventually lead a separate life.

Tiger—Ox

Here we find a karmic power struggle. The Tiger's outgoing personality leaves the Ox in the shadows more often than not, and this can embitter the Ox (who soon tires of the Tiger's perpetual place in the spotlight).

Tiger—Tiger

This combination is like two captains fighting at the wheel while the crew watches them in their exhaustive struggle for top position. While many of the signs cohabit peacefully with those of their own sign, two Tigers are an exception.

Tiger—Rabbit

The Tiger's energy level and verve tend to bulldoze the easily overwhelmed Rabbit. The Tiger is boisterous, while the Rabbit is understated. The Tiger is as fearless as the Rabbit is faint-hearted. There are much better matches for each of these two.

Tiger—Dragon

This is a sturdy relationship that can stand the test of time. These two sources of power are capable of completing vast projects and formulating visionary plans of action. The Tiger and the Dragon are, above all, good friends.

Tiger—Snake

The action-oriented Tiger is annoyed by the Snake's slow deliberations in life. Tigers move fast, think fast, and intend to cross life's finish line first. The Snake takes their time in everything they do. The Tiger may perceive this trait as laziness.

Tiger—Horse

These two kindred souls are natural friends and lovers. Likeminded in their pursuit of new challenges, the Tiger and Horse speak the same language of action, idealism, and improving the human condition.

Tiger—Goat

To be perfectly blunt, the Tiger is strong and independent, while the Goat is weak and very dependent. The Goat's lack of ambition and slothful ways infuriate most Tigers.

Tiger—Monkey

There can be a trust issue between these two polarized souls. The Tiger has no patience for the foolishness of the Monkey's schemes and tricks. This pairing makes better friends than lovers.

Tiger—Rooster

These two souls have problems communicating, and more than likely this is an infatuation rather than a long-term union. The Tiger and the Rooster are "firecracker" personalities, and the union of these two can spark some memorable verbal battles.

Tiger—Dog

If ever there were a karmic love affair, it would be between these two souls. The Tiger and the Dog are naturally drawn toward one another and interact with encouragement and generosity. The Tiger is the emperor and the Dog their prime minister.

Tiger—Pig

While the Tiger is supremely compatible with both the Horse and the Dog, it is the honest and affectionate Pig who is the Tiger's soul mate. The resigned Pig is never threatened by the Tiger's grand accomplishments and truly appreciates their sublime qualities. In friendship and in love, this relationship is a keeper.

The Rabbit and Love

Streetwise yet gentle, charming Rabbit souls are artistic albeit aloof lovers. Many a patient partner has tried to coax, convince, and persuade a Rabbit into giving up their much-prized freedom in exchange for the domestic life. It is characteristic of Rabbits to be attracted to both older and younger admirers and lovers. While wanting to remain independent, Rabbits do enjoy being cared for, pampered, and protected. This can send mixed messages, and ultimately throw the course of love off balance. Rabbits prefer to keep their options open; however, once committed they are devoted and supportive partners. Rabbits are charming, gentle, and somewhat passive lovers who find it difficult to fall in love due to a desire for virtue and a quest for perfection.

Romantically, the best match for the Rabbit is with those born during Goat or Pig years; however; their true soul mate is found with the devoted Dog. Rabbits are wise to be cautious in love relationships with Dragons or Roosters.

Rabbit—Rat

The Rabbit is not as invested in the relationship as their Rat partner is and can become emotionally unavailable. This pairing makes better friends than lovers. Both share a love of the fine arts and scholarly pursuits.

Rabbit—Ox

These two are solitary loners by nature. The Rabbit can suffer from a lack of romance with the Ox. The Oxen's brand of love is stable and practical, while the Rabbit needs luxury, romance, and pampering.

Rabbit—Tiger

The Rabbit can be overwhelmed by the Tiger's brusque ways. The Rabbit is a good friend and adviser to the Tiger, but there are better matches for each of these two.

Rabbit—Rabbit

Two Rabbits in tandem would keep a museum curator on his toes. This is a gentle combination of kindred spirits and an auspicious partnership in both friendship and love. Together they create an eternal party and enjoy many a fireside chat.

Rabbit—Dragon

Unfortunately, the Rabbit and the Dragon are only one sign (and many times only one year) apart and can be thrown together as classmates, colleagues, and spouses. The Rabbit is refined and mannerly, while the Dragon is crass and outspoken. This creates many tensions.

Rabbit—Snake

The Rabbit and the Snake are equally polished, and these two creative and philosophical souls enjoy one another's company. However, despite sharing a taste for the finer things in life, they will experience a difficult union. The Snake has the potential to consume the Rabbit.

Rabbit—Horse

These two always have an enjoyable time together, and the Rabbit doesn't mind staying home and enjoying their privacy while the Horse conquers new pastures. This pairing works as a good friendship and workable union.

Rabbit—Goat

These two are best friends and speak a similar language of propriety and creativity, and they walk hand-in-hand on the road toward enlightenment. In their quest to find and create beauty in this life, the Rabbit and the Goat form a melodious union.

Rabbit—Monkey

Rabbits find Monkeys a little too superficial for their taste. The Monkey can't resist tricking the Rabbit, but the Rabbit is prepared with some tricks of its own. This is not a beneficial relationship for either sign.

Rabbit—Rooster

No matter how hard these two try, compatibility seems beyond their reach. The brash Rooster's caustic criticism sets the Rabbit's nerves on edge. While relationships between all signs are possible, this combination of souls is almost always a recipe for disaster.

Rabbit—Dog

These two souls recognize each other immediately, and most have karmic links from other times and places. If the "attached" Dog and the "detached" Rabbit can overcome their fears and trust issues, this is a match made in heaven.

Rabbit—Pig

This is a sweet relationship between two gentle souls. Both are well-mannered and genuinely virtuous. The diplomatic and socially adept Rabbit aids and befriends the shy Pig to the benefit of both. These two are unmistakably good partners.

The Dragon and Love

A lucky star shines on those souls born into Dragon years, especially in matters of the heart. Dragons possess a mixture of passion and enthusiasm and will stimulate their partner's spirit of competition and taste for the finer things in life. This is a soul who knows what they are doing and what they seek to obtain. Possessing a taste for the unusual and the diverse, Dragons can be easily infatuated and savor many partners. In love, Dragons are autonomous and will rarely put their life on hold for romance. Their choice of a marriage partner is inspired by a deep need to be respected and admired. Never in a hurry to marry, Dragons enjoy legions of admirers, but may choose to remain single or marry later in life.

Romantically, the best match for the Dragon is with those born during Rat or Monkey years. However, their true soul mate is found with the candid Rooster. The Dragon should be cautious in love relationships with the Dog and Rabbit.

Dragon—Rat

Both of these souls recognize each other's taste for variety. When married, emotional security reigns supreme, and the Dragon and the

Rat work as a team. They share a love of socializing, and the Rat will never upstage their cherished Dragon.

Dragon—Ox

A clash of wills prevents any long-term relationship between these two. Both the Dragon and Ox need admiration, and it is not forthcoming from either. Well-defined roles and mutual respect is critical for any relationship between them.

Dragon—Tiger

This pairing creates a sturdy (though somewhat high-drama) relationship between these two. Both are powerful and willful souls, yet they are able to work together, play together, and love together.

Dragon—Rabbit

The Dragon bowls the Rabbit over with their force of will and overbearing conduct. The Rabbit is courteous and gracious, while the Dragon is direct and blunt, causing the Rabbit embarrassment.

Dragon—Dragon

This "Priest" and "Priestess" couple of the Chinese Zodiac is an amazing pair. This is an extreme union both positively and negatively. Each must hold the other in the highest esteem, and they each must have their own stage on which to shine.

Dragon—Snake

This is a relationship that has the potential for happiness if the possessive Snake will allow the autonomous Dragon to leave the lair from time to time. Infidelity could become an issue with this couple; yet if the union is severed, they will continue to remain friends.

Dragon—Horse

There is a profound clash of egos between the self-assured Dragon and the self-absorbed Horse. Both prefer to be center stage and neither is prepared to bow to the other. This is a superficial relationship at best.

Dragon—Goat

This unlikely pairing can work wonderfully if the Dragon is male and the Goat is female. The Dragon must use delicacy and gentleness to keep from overwhelming their Goat. This is a strong and lasting attraction.

Dragon—Monkey

These two compatible souls seek each other out and speak a similar language of unpredictability, irrepressibility, and innovation. The Dragon and Monkey have an excellent chance for a stimulating and enduring relationship.

Dragon—Rooster

These two soul mates are a match made in heaven. The Rooster has the pluck and audacity to hold the interest of the bold Dragon. Together they make a handsome and lively couple.

Dragon—Dog

This is an interesting relationship, to say the least. Being polarized opposites, the Dragon and the Dog are as different as night and day. However, each possesses traits that the other would do well to learn. They are better as colleagues than lovers.

Dragon—Pig

Almost everyone gets along well with the sweet-natured Pig, and the Dragon is no exception. A wide and smooth path to romance awaits these two. However, the Dragon must vow never to cheat the trusting Pig.

The Snake and Love

Snake souls are sensual and impassioned lovers. Their method of seduction is an arousing mixture of attractiveness, sensuality, and intuition. Snake souls have a magical quality of well-mannered charm, fascinating insights, and irresistible sexuality. In love, Snakes are both jealous and possessive, craving sleepless nights of passionate caresses and intimate secrets. This is a lover who desires to be totally merged with their partner, knowing the most intimate details of their lover's soul. Immersed and enmeshed on a deep level when in love, a Snake intuitively kindles, feeds, and fans love's fire. Snakes choose their partners cautiously, allowing the relationship to slowly accumulate energy and longevity.

Romantically, the best match for the Snake is with those born during Ox or Rooster years. However, their true soul mate is found with the mercurial Monkey. The Snake should be cautious in love relationships with the Tiger and Pig.

Snake—Rat

The Rat is a sensual master, and sex is something they are capable of surrendering to completely. The Snake, however, has the ability to devour the Rat, body and soul. The Rat may suffer heartache in this relationship.

Snake—Ox

These two best friends have a deep understanding of each other. This pairing has excellent compatibility in friendship and in marriage. These two like-minded souls can form a union of long duration.

Snake—Tiger

The Snake's slow, calculating, and endless pondering of the meaning of life annoys and frustrates the Tiger. The Snake feels pushed and prodded to act faster than they are comfortable. Snakes would be wise to look for a less-impulsive partner.

Snake—Rabbit

Sharing a taste for luxury and the finer things in life, the Snake and Rabbit could very well find themselves together. However, the Snake is always in charge of the relationship's direction. The Snake may or may not choose to consume the Rabbit.

Snake—Dragon

If the possessive Snake can allow the autonomous Dragon to leave the lair from time to time, this pairing will proceed smoothly. If the Snake constricts the Dragon's movement, there will be difficulties.

Snake—Snake

This is a lovely relationship steeped in beauty, elegance, and otherworldly knowledge. Nonetheless, a double dose of the passive, negative, feminine yin energy leaves each person wanting the other to take the lead. Expect a long, contemplative courtship.

Snake—Horse

Mutual respect and intense physical attraction make this a workable union. However, the hurdles that the Horse must jump are external, in contrast to the Snake's mainly internal world. This can erect a fence between the two souls.

Snake—Goat

These two very "yin" souls need to attach themselves to a strong wagon that does much of the pulling for them. It is a chilly relationship with too much emotional distance and no one to take the lead.

Snake—Monkey

These unlikely soul mates have the potential to celebrate a golden wedding anniversary. Equally matched in both guile and allure, the Snake and the Monkey will seldom tire of their intense physical attraction to each other. Beware of infidelities that can derail the union.

Snake—Rooster

This is a winning combination of wisdom and work. The philosophical Snake and the industrious Rooster speak a common language of conservatism, method, and physical appearance. Still, the Rooster is an early riser while the Snake prefers to languish until noon.

Snake—Dog

These two souls never run out of interesting topics to discuss and are first-rate friends. They both seek to understand the metaphysics of life, and each soul tends to be multisensorial. They will enjoy many hours together delving into otherworldly knowledge.

Snake—Pig

While both are decent and deeply feeling souls, the Snake and the Pig remain in polarized opposition. The Pig judges the Snake to be less than honest, and this can drive a wedge between the two. The Snake, meanwhile, often tires of the Pig's Pollyannaish naiveté.

The Horse and Love

Horse souls value their freedom absolutely. They are physically attractive, intense, and enchanting lovers who are difficult to tame. Those who love a Horse must also be lovers of challenge and adventure. Sentimental, impatient, and ardent for love, the Horse seeks to overwhelm (and to be thunderstruck in the process). These souls can be easily infatuated and fall prey to immediate attractions. Passionate and vulnerable to just the right smile, the Horse lives according to the rhythms of their heart. They love with their entire being and are never short on conversation. Eager to discuss and to hear their lover's opinions, active and energetic Horses are affectionate and entertaining companions.

Romantically, the best match for the Horse is with those born during Tiger or Horse years. However, their true soul mate is found with the fun-loving Goat. Horses would be wise to be cautious in love relationships with the Rat and Ox.

Horse—Rat

Interestingly, despite their direct opposition, these souls tend to frequently attract one another. Rats need an understanding ear to listen to their ideas, while the Horse is too preoccupied with their own dreams and ambitions. This relationship can end in bitterness.

Horse—Ox

The Horse would rather be anyplace except home. This is nothing less than treason to the Ox who holds the family circle in reverence. The Horse interprets the Oxen's stability as authority, and neither sign has the foggiest idea of how the other thinks and feels.

Horse—Tiger

These two are natural friends and lovers. Each supports the other in their mutual pursuit of making the world a better place. Both are physically active, athletic, and in forward yang motion.

Horse—Rabbit

The Rabbit doesn't mind staying home and enjoying their privacy while the Horse conquers new pastures. This pairing makes an enjoyable friendship and amiable union. The Horse's yang energy is in harmony with the Rabbit's yin soul.

Horse—Dragon

This is an ego clash of epic proportions, as both the Horse and the Dragon vie for attention and audience approval. These two will seldom acquiesce to share the limelight, and neither will compromise with the other. This is a difficult relationship.

Horse—Snake

Mutual respect and intense physical attraction make this a workable union. However, the hurdles that the Horse yearns to jump are external in contrast to the Snakes mainly internal world. This can erect a fence between the two.

Horse—Horse

Similar to their Tiger brothers and sisters, two Horse souls are just too much of a good thing. The double yang and Fire element can make for a stampede through life. If these two independent souls team up, much time may be spent apart.

Horse—Goat

These two soul mates compliment each other perfectly. The Horse is the very personification of the yang (positive) day force; the Goat is the absolute essence of the yin (negative) night force. Together these two make up a perfect whole.

Horse—Monkey

This is a relationship that challenges every bit of the Monkey's ingenuity and artfulness. If the clever Monkey can convince the Horse that life with them will be unique, this can work quite nicely. With this combination the Monkey tends to pursue the Horse.

Horse—Rooster

This is a difficult pairing of energies, and neither feels a strong enough bond to make any sacrifices for the other. The Rooster's fussiness leaves the Horse feeling tense and nervous. This is an apathetic relationship in friendship and in love.

Horse—Dog

The Dog and the Horse comprise a remarkable couple. These two souls adore each other and speak the same language of feelings, family, and fairness. These exceptional humanitarians may very well find themselves in the limelight.

Horse—Pig

Surprisingly, the normally peace-loving Pig can become antagonistic and quarrelsome when paired with the Horse. The Pig feels it necessary to correct the Horse, and generally rains on the Horse's parade.

The Goat and Love

In personal relations with the Goat, the key words are propriety and delicacy. In love, the easy-going Goat can give a great deal, but will expect much in exchange, especially monetarily. The Goat likes to be comfortably taken care of while they create the beautiful and aesthetic in life. The Goat needs a partner who will manage the mundane, day-to-day aspects of life. Hours spent filling out income tax forms is not for them. This sensitive and aesthetic soul has impeccable taste and uses this ability to create an artistic and comfortable love nest. Beautiful surroundings, ballets, works of art, music, and poetry are what romance is made of for Goats. Goats are romantics who desire declarations of love and slow seductions before engaging in physical pleasures.

Romantically, the best match for the Goat is with those born during Rabbit or Pig years. However, their true soul mate is found with the enthusiastic Horse. Goats would be wise to cautiously approach love relationships with the Ox and Rat.

Goat—Rat

This relationship is a difficult one. The Rat is an early riser, and the Goat is not. These two seem to have many interests in common, but the way in which each views the world is radically different. This pairing makes better friends than lovers.

Goat—Ox

If one says black, the other says white. These two polarized opposites can make sparks fly with their radically different temperaments and opinions. Oxen are predictable and responsible, but the Goat interprets this as a tyrannical prison of sorts.

Goat—Tiger

This combination of souls can have its pleasant moments, but friction is the usual result. The fearless Tiger will bulldoze right over the sensitive Goat. These two can have fun as social acquaintances, but marriage may prove too difficult.

Goat—Rabbit

In their quest to find and create beauty in this life, the Rabbit and the Goat form a melodious union. These two best friends walk hand-in-hand through a world of aesthetics, culture, and refinement.

Goat—Dragon

This unusual pairing can work nicely if the Dragon doesn't over-whelm the Goat. While a strong and lasting attraction can ensue from a pairing of these two signs, the Goat will often have trouble keeping their balance through the Dragon's hot and cold moods.

Goat—Snake

These two very "yin" souls need to attach themselves to a strong wagon that does much of the pulling for them. This is a chilly relation-ship with too much emotional distance and no one to take the lead.

Goat—Horse

These two soul mates compliment each other perfectly. The Horse is the very personification of the yang, positive day force; the Goat is the absolute essence of the yin, negative night force. Together these two make up a perfect whole.

Goat—Goat

This pair is a picnic amongst the clouds. These two "Good Samaritans" enjoy each other's company and share a sensitivity to beauty and balance. Two Goats should be cautious, however, in the handling of their finances. There will be no competition between these fortunate and romantic souls.

Goat—Monkey

The Goat and the Monkey are often immediately attracted to one another and get along famously—for a while. The Monkey will enjoy the Goat's fortunate financial position until the price becomes too high to pay. However, if the money runs out, many times the Monkey will also.

Goat—Rooster

This is a challenging relationship of leisure clashing with hard work. The Rooster's prodding and pushing of the Goat to be more productive is not favorable for harmony between the two.

Goat—Dog

Both of these souls tend to be pessimistic and prone to melancholy. A double dose of cynicism does neither the anxious Dog nor the depressive Goat any good. The Dog herds the Goat into places they have no desire to go, thus bringing out the billy goat's horns.

Goat—Pig

A loving relationship of courtesy and respect exists between these two gentle souls. The Goat teaches the Pig about romance and, in turn, learns temperance from the Pig. A winning combination both as friends and lovers.

The Monkey and Love

According to Chinese legend, the Monkey is the everlasting child and eternally youthful soul of the Chinese Zodiac. Monkeys are witty and amusing lovers, but romantically they can have difficult love relationships due to their complex personalities and suspicious nature. Restless and sexually curious, Monkeys possess an effervescent character that shines in social situations, becomes infatuated easily, and can quickly become bored. Monkeys are imaginative and have an unequivocal need for variety. They are full of passion, humor, and restlessness. They are also hard to tie down, communicative, progressive, and performance-oriented. These souls are self-starters and take the initiative in love. The Monkey will offer an appealing future to their beloved, one that is rich in play and amusement.

Romantically, the best match for the Monkey is with those born during Rat or Dragon years. However, their true soul mate is found with the sage Snake. Monkeys are warned to be cautious in love relationships with the Tiger and Pig.

Monkey—Rat

Sexuality is a pleasure and a gift between Rats and Monkeys. These two love each other and are not bashful about it. Nights of love intertwined with intellectual stimulation await this pair.

Monkey—Ox

Because of their self-sufficient and practical nature, love and sex are important (but not absolutely essential) to Oxen. This dampens the Monkey's enthusiasm, and often results in resentment.

Monkey—Tiger

These two opposite souls distrust each other. The Tiger knows that the Monkey is capable of playing tricks and gaining confidences, and this "know it all" attitude sets the Tiger's nerves on edge.

Monkey—Rabbit

The Rabbit passes the buck to the capable Monkey and does not wish to assume responsibility for the outcome of situations. The Monkey can't resist tricking the Rabbit, but the Rabbit is prepared to make a quick getaway.

Monkey—Dragon

These two compatible souls flow together naturally and are kindred spirits. Each brings to this union many unanticipated and new methods.

The Dragon and Monkey have an excellent chance for an enduring relationship.

Monkey—Snake

These unlikely soul mates will seldom tire of their intense physical attraction to each other. The Snake must not be stingy with the Monkey, who can become depressed.

Monkey—Horse

This is a relationship that challenges every bit of the Monkey's ingenuity and artfulness. If the clever Monkey can convince the Horse that life with them will be unique, this can work quite nicely.

Monkey—Goat

The Goat and the Monkey are immediately attracted to one another and get along famously for a while. The Monkey often enjoys the Goat's fortunate financial position, until following the Goat's rules and moods becomes too high of a price to pay.

Monkey—Monkey

This is another harmonious same-sign match. These two souls are a handful together, and result in a carnival of ideas and fun. There should be caution regarding third parties entering the union.

Monkey—Rooster

This is a pairing that can bring rewards to both sides. The lively debates between these two cause others to label it a love/hate relationship, but the relationship works admirably for each one.

Monkey—Dog

The Monkey is one of the few signs who can lift the Dog out of its frequent bouts of doom and gloom. Able to see life as a comedy, the Monkey offers the Dog both friendship and love.

Monkey—Pig

Considering the surprising regularity that these two souls come together, the natural assumption would be that they are compatible. This is rarely the case, however, as the tricky Monkey can't resist misleading the naive Pig.

The Rooster and Love

In love, the Rooster is flirtatious and enjoys an open and confident disposition. Their love partner will need some credible credentials to capture the Rooster's heart. Roosters thrive on compliments, and have an emotional and possessive nature in matters of the heart. Because of their restless anxiety and impatience, they tend to be attracted to those who are secure, patient, and caring. Roosters are candid critics, and they love lively debates. According to Chinese legend, the Rooster is highly sexual, very fertile, and may have an above-average number of children. Romantic displays of emotion are difficult for this conservative soul. They need a partner who is as capable and outspoken as they are, and someone who possesses a superbly sarcastic sense of humor.

Romantically, the best match for the Rooster is with those born during Ox and Snake years. However, their true soul mate is found with the self-confident Dragon. Roosters should be cautious in love relationships with the Dog and Rabbit.

Rooster—Rat

Rats and Roosters are equally interactive, and can always expect lively discussions. However, a combative relationship ensues when the Rat criticizes the Rooster and points out their shortcomings. This pairing can maintain a good friendship, but a long-term relationship may not endure.

Rooster—Ox

The Ox delights in the company of the efficient Rooster, whether it is a female Ox keeping the home fires burning for her military Rooster husband, or a male Ox enjoying his "little firecracker" Rooster of a wife efficiently running their home. This is a match destined to last.

Rooster—Tiger

These two souls have problems communicating. More than likely, this pairing is destined to be a brief affair rather than a long-term union. The Tiger and the Rooster are both "skyrocket" personalities, and the union of these two can spark some memorable clashes.

Rooster—Rabbit

Despite effort on the part of each, compatibility seems beyond the reach of the Rooster and Rabbit. The Rooster considers the Rabbit a "weak sister," too delicate and easily hurt. This is not an auspicious relationship.

Rooster—Dragon

The Rooster has the backbone and brass to hold the interest of the confident Dragon. Together they make a handsome and lively couple. These two soul mates could celebrate a golden wedding anniversary

Rooster—Snake

The philosophical Snake and the industrious Rooster speak a common language of control, calculation, and attractive appearance. However, the Rooster is busier, faster-working, and more aggressive than the pensive, deep-thinking Snake.

Rooster—Horse

The Rooster's fussiness leaves the Horse feeling tense and nervous. This is often an apathetic relationship in friendship and in love.

It is a difficult pairing of energies, and neither feels a strong enough bond to make any sacrifices for the other.

Rooster—Goat

This is a challenging relationship of industry clashing with sloth. The Rooster prods and pushes the Goat to be more productive. The Goat feels tyrannized, and is likely to rebel.

Rooster—Monkey

This is an auspicious coupling that brings rewards to both sides. The lively debates between these two sometimes resemble a love/hate relationship, but the relationship works well in the long run.

Rooster—Rooster

Whether a showy peacock or a gentle hen, these two souls will rarely cohabit peacefully. The term "cockfight" is often used to describe the interaction between two plucky Roosters.

Rooster—Dog

This is a difficult combination of energies, and should a verbal brawl break out between these two, take cover! Each sign antagonizes the other, and a relationship is likely to bring out the worst in both personalities.

Rooster—Pig

This is a blissful relationship full of sincere admiration between both parties. The Rooster will benefit from the Pig's wisdom and presence of mind, while the Pig offers the Rooster respect and admiration.

The Dog and Love

Love is a sober subject for the Dog, and they are never nonchalant in matters of the heart. The Dog approaches love with earnestness, and they are on an endless quest to find their soul mate in this life. They desperately seek a partner who understands the deep anxiety and seriousness that pervades their soul. The Dog withers without tenderness, yet they can have trouble expressing their own buried affections. The Dog's brand of love is earthy and passionate. However, the heart-wrenching howl of a betrayed or rejected Dog can make any bite seem innocuous. A Dog has difficulty letting go of relationships, and difficult partners respect them for their patience and loyalty.

Romantically, the best match for the Dog is with those born during Tiger or Horse years. However, their true soul mate is found with the diplomatic Rabbit. They should proceed cautiously in love relationships with the Dragon and Rooster.

Dog—Rat

The Rat can't help correcting the Dog's all too human errors, and the Dog feels belittled and not up to par— a disaster from an insecure Dog's point of view. This relationship too closely resembles a parent/child relationship to ever work smoothly.

Dog—Ox

This could be a maudlin pity party waiting to happen, and a double dose of pessimism does neither of these two souls any good. However, the Dog has much compassion for the sweet-natured (yet awkward) Ox, and this can be a nurturing and loyal relationship.

Dog—Tiger

If ever there were a karmic love affair, it would be between these two souls. The Tiger and the Dog are naturally drawn toward one another, and they interact with encouragement and generosity. The Tiger is the emperor, and the Dog the prime minister.

Dog—Rabbit

This is a match made in heaven, and these two souls recognize each other immediately. This match is so potent that if something were to go wrong between them and a separation ensued, neither would likely recover fully. A soul mate connection of cosmic proportions.

Dog—Dragon

Being polarized opposites, the Dragon and the Dog are as different as night and day. However, each possesses traits that the other would do well to learn. This pairing makes for good business associates, but a difficult and complicated love union.

Dog—Snake

Both of these signs seek to understand the metaphysics of life, and each soul tends to be multisensory. They can enjoy many hours together, delving into otherworldly knowledge. These two souls never run out of interesting topics to discuss and are first-rate friends.

Dog—Horse

The Dog and the Horse make a delightful team in friendship and in love. These two souls adore one another and speak the same language of humanity, freedom, and fairness. These two Robin Hoods may find themselves in the middle of a revolution.

Dog—Goat

A double dose of cynicism does neither the anxious Dog nor the depressive Goat any good. The Dog herds the Goat into places they have no desire to go, thus bringing out the billy goat's horns. Both souls tend to be pessimists and are prone to expect the worst.

Dog—Monkey

The Monkey's superb sense of humor and absurdity lifts the Dog out of its frequent bouts of doom and gloom. However, the Monkey can be wickedly naughty, sexually speaking, and the Dog would rarely forgive such an indiscretion.

Dog—Rooster

In this pairing, each sign often antagonizes the other, and a relationship is likely to bring out the worst in both personalities. This is a difficult combination of energies, as the thin-skinned Dog is not equipped to be the recipient of the Rooster's caustic barbs.

Dog—Dog

These two serious souls are very compatible together. Each examines the other through the glass of proven loyalty. Each functions as a confidant, and both are well equipped to support the other through times of anxiety and worry.

Dog—Pig

These two tender souls, while not found in the traditional triangles of compatibility, can share a long and happy life together. This pairing makes a loyal and romantic allegiance—one that is able to stand the test of time.

The Pig and Love

The Pig is a most sensual soul who needs tenderness and physical demonstrations of love. Pig souls without a soul mate or lover will deeply withdraw into themselves. The Pig is a deeply feeling person who is devoted to their mate and able to overlook their loved one's inadequacies. The Pig's heart is simple and pure. Holding the last love position in the Zodiac (which carries the link to the astrological new cycle), the Pig is gifted at joining fragmented emotions, and mending and comforting broken hearts.

Monogamous and long-suffering in love, the Pig is an honest and supportive mate who can be counted on for better or for worse.

Romantically, the best match for the Pig is with those born during Goat or Rabbit years. However, their true soul mate is found with the brave Tiger. They are wise to be cautious in love relationships with the Snake and the Monkey.

Pig—Rat

Rats have a tendency to feel as if nobody understands them. Feeling understood in a love relationship is important for their peace of mind, and the compassionate Pig fits the emotional bill.

Pig—Ox

These two calm souls speak the same language of quiet strength and old-fashioned virtues. However, the Ox and Pig do not normally gravitate to each other, each being quiet and solitary souls. Unless introduced by a third party, romantic sparks may never ignite between the two.

Pig—Tiger

While the Tiger is awesomely compatible with both the Horse and the Dog, it is the honest and affectionate Pig who is the Tiger's soul mate. The resigned Pig is never threatened by the Tiger's grand accomplishments, and they truly appreciate the Tiger's sublime qualities. In both friendship and in love, this relationship is a keeper.

Pig—Rabbit

This is a sweet relationship between two gentle souls. Both are well mannered and genuinely virtuous. The diplomatic and socially adept Rabbit often aids and befriends the shy Pig, to the benefit of both. These two are unmistakably good partners.

Pig—Dragon

Almost everyone gets along well with the sweet-natured Pig, and the Dragon is no exception. A wide and smooth path to romance awaits these two.

Pig—Snake

While both are agreeable and deeply feeling souls, the Snake and the Pig remain in polarized opposition. The Pig judges the Snake to be less than scrupulous, and this can drive a wedge between the two. In addition, the Snake will eventually tire of the Pig's over-optimism.

Pig—Horse

The normally peace-loving Pig can become antagonistic and quarrelsome when paired with the Horse. The Pig feels it necessary to correct the Horse, and generally throws a wet blanket on the Horse's parade. .

Pig—Goat

A loving relationship of courtesy and respect exists between these two gentle souls. The Goat teaches the Pig about romance and in turn, learns temperance from the Pig. Both are Good Samaritans and will casually take life as it comes.

Pig—Monkey

With the regularity that these two souls come together, the natural assumption would be that they are compatible. Unfortunately, this is not the case. The Monkey often has an agenda of its own, which may or may not include the Pig. The Pig stands to get hurt in this union.

Pig—Rooster

This is a great relationship. Good humor and admiration are found between the Pig and the Rooster. The Rooster will benefit from the Pig's even temperament, while the Pig encourages the Rooster to express its hidden feelings in safety.

Pig—Dog

These two tender souls, while not found in the traditional triangles of compatibility, often celebrate golden wedding anniversaries. This is a loyal and devoted couple able to stand the test of time.

Pig—Pig

Two Pigs are akin to a committee of ethics and morals. While no human is perfect, these two come very close. Both are honest, uncomplicated, and desire to fully enjoy the sensual pleasures in life.

Chapter 18

Quick Reference Guide to the 12 Signs of the Eastern Zodiac

The Charming Rat (Tze)

January 31, 1900 to February 18, 1901: Metal Rat

February 18, 1912 to February 5, 1913: Water Rat

February 5, 1924 to January 24, 1925: Wood Rat

January 24, 1936 to February 10, 1937: Fire Rat

February 10, 1948 to January 28, 1949: Earth Rat

January 28, 1960 to February 14, 1961: Metal Rat

February 15, 1972 to February 2, 1973: Water Rat

February 2, 1984 to February 19, 1985: Wood Rat

February 19, 1996 to February 6, 1997: Fire Rat

February 7, 2008 to January 25, 2009: Earth Rat

The socially adept Rat possesses charisma, charm, intelligence, and the ability to verbally exchange their eclectic knowledge. Both sociable and romantic, and armed with complex emotions, those born into this sign of the Eastern Zodiac form deep emotional ties with others. The always thrifty Rat counts their pennies and knows how to spot a bargain. Impatient with those of slower wit or actions, this soul needs a bright partner who is willing to lend an ear, and who possesses a good sense of humor. The talkative Rat is also a natural writer and critic, with an eye for details. High-strung, curious, and ever alert to their environment, the essence of this curious and intellectual sign is "concealment." Rats gather strength between the hours of 11 p.m. and 1 a.m.

Famous Rats:

Jules Verne
Truman Capote
Eugene O'Neill
William Shakespeare
Hugh Grant
Antonio Banderas
Cameron Diaz
Prince Charles

The Stable Ox (Chou)

February 19, 1901 to February 7, 1902: Metal Ox
February 6, 1913 to January 25, 1914: Water Ox
January 25, 1925 to February 12, 1926: Wood Ox
February 11, 1937 to January 30, 1938: Fire Ox
January 29, 1949 to February 16, 1950: Earth Ox
February 15, 1961 to February 4, 1962: Metal Ox
February 3, 1973 to January 22, 1974: Water Ox
February 20, 1985 to February 8, 1986: Wood Ox
February 7, 1997 to January 27, 1998: Fire Ox
January 26, 2009 to February 13, 2010: Earth Ox

The Ox (or Buffalo) is the hard-working, serious loner of the family. Their essence is "endurance." The opinionated Ox is determined, strong, and conservative, and possesses a notable gift of manual dexterity. Family and duty are of the utmost importance to the homespun Ox. Souls born under this second sign of the Zodiac are capable of leading nations and running a most efficient household. Oxen are powerful individuals with stubborn, reliable personalities. Whether at home or at work, these souls need to be the captain of their ship. They are dependable, honest, and stable. The quiet yet firm Ox is easy-going, but possesses an intense passion beneath their calm exterior. The industrious Ox needs a partner of substance and loyalty. Oxen gather strength during the quiet hours between 1 a.m. and 3 a.m.

Famous Oxen:

George Clooney

Princess Diana of Wales

Bill O'Reilly

Saddam Hussein

Jack Nicholson

Meg Ryan

Bill Cosby

Napoleon

The Courageous Tiger (Yin)

February 8, 1902 to January 28, 1903: Water Tiger

January 26, 1914 to February 13, 1915: Wood Tiger

February 13, 1926 to February 1, 1927: Fire Tiger

January 31, 1938 to February 18, 1939: Earth Tiger

February 17, 1950 to February 5, 1951: Metal Tiger

February 5, 1962 to January 24, 1963: Water Tiger

January 23, 1974 to February 10, 1975: Wood Tiger

February 9, 1986 to January 28, 1987: Fire Tiger

January 28, 1998 to February 15, 1999: Earth Tiger

February 14, 2010 to February 2, 2011: Metal Tiger

The Tiger is the restless, adventurous, and always courageous risk-taker of the Chinese Zodiac. With a sense of "empowered entitlement," nobility and humanitarian causes appeal to the generous Tiger. These souls are tenderhearted and affectionate with their friends and family, yet self-reliant and fiercely independent. This is the most unpredictable of the 12 signs, and they are blessed with charm, nerve, and grand ideas. Tigers flash brilliantly through life, sometimes without caution for their own security. Fearless, enthusiastic, and optimistic, the passionate Tiger is an unconventional yet humanitarian soul. The noble Tiger needs a sexy, exciting partner who will forever remain a challenge. They gather their legendary strength between 3 a.m. and 5 a.m., the predawn hours they rule.

Famous Tigers:

Tom Cruise
"Crocodile Hunter" Steve Irwin
Demi Moore
Rosie O'Donnell
Jerry Lewis
Hugh Hefner
Michelle Yeoh
Leonardo DiCaprio

The Discreet Rabbit (Mao)

February 14, 1915 to February 2, 1916: Wood Rabbit
January 29, 1903 to February 15, 1904: Water Rabbit
February 2, 1927 to January 22, 1928: Fire Rabbit
February 19, 1939 to February 7, 1940: Earth Rabbit
February 6, 1951 to January 26, 1952: Metal Rabbit
January 25, 1963 to February 12, 1964: Water Rabbit
February 11, 1975 to January 30, 1976: Wood Rabbit
January 29, 1987 to February 16, 1988: Fire Rabbit
February 16. 1999 to February 4, 2000: Earth Rabbit
February 3, 2011 to January 22, 2012: Metal Rabbit

The well-mannered Rabbit is diplomatic, easygoing, refined, and a devoted friend. Detached and aloof, the Rabbit often flees personal upheaval and disruption. These souls excel in the fine arts, and are highly creative. Well-grounded and ever virtuous, Rabbits shun risk and emotional entanglements, choosing instead security and quiet stability. Business partners extraordinaire, the peaceful and contented Rabbit possesses a quiet sensuality and the gift of self-preservation. Sensitive and easily hurt, the private Rabbit keeps their own counsel and is highly sought after for their advice. The ethical Rabbit needs a loving and unselfish partner who makes very little demands on their time and privacy. Rabbits gather strength during the early dawn hours they rule, between 5 a.m. and 7 a.m.

Famous Rabbits:

Confucius
Henry Kissinger
Brad Pitt
Bob Hope
Frank Sinatra
Queen Elizabeth
Nicholas Cage
Jet Li

The Outspoken Dragon (Chen)

February 16, 1904 to February 3, 1905: Wood Dragon
February 3, 1916 to January 22, 1917: Fire Dragon
January 23, 1928 to February 9, 1929: Earth Dragon
February 8, 1940 to January 26, 1941: Metal Dragon
January 27, 1952 to February 13, 1953: Water Dragon
February 13, 1964 to February 1, 1965: Wood Dragon
January 31, 1976 to February 17, 1977: Fire Dragon
February 17, 1988 to February 5, 1989: Earth Dragon
February 5, 2000 to January 23, 2001: Metal Dragon
January 23, 2012 to February 9, 2013: Water Dragon

The powerful Dragon is the physically healthy, sentimental visionary of the Chinese Zodiac. Outspoken, lucky, and financially fortunate, Dragons display boundless energy and vitality. These proud souls do not like to be challenged, and their nature is that of "unpredictability." Egotistic and always high-profile, Dragons are assertive, boisterous, and extroverted personalities. Successful and popular, this fifth sign of the Zodiac is born to be in the public eye, and often produces excellent actors and performers. Original, enthusiastic, and healthy, the ardent Dragon needs a strong and intriguing partner, or else they may opt to live a solitary life. The Dragon gathers strength between the morning hours of 7 a.m. and 9 a.m.

Famous Dragons:

Tom Jones

Alicia Silverstone

Dan Aykroyd

Liam Nielsen

Sandra Bullock

Calista Flockhart

Joseph Campbell

Robin Williams

The Philosophical Snake (Si)

February 4, 1905 to January 24, 1906: Wood Snake

January 23, 1917 to February 10, 1918: Fire Snake

February 10, 1929 to January 29, 1930: Earth Snake

January 27, 1941 to February 14, 1942: Metal Snake

February 14, 1953 to February 2, 1954: Water Snake

February 2, 1965 to January 20, 1966: Wood Snake

February 18, 1977 to February 6, 1978: Fire Snake

February 6, 1989 to January 26, 1990: Earth Snake

January 24, 2001 to February 11, 2002: Metal Snake

February 10, 2013 to January 30, 2014: Water Snake

The Snake is the wise philosopher and stealthy personality of the Chinese Zodiac. Physically attractive, with satin skin and impeccable advice, the Snakes are the sages, psychiatrists, and spiritual advisors of the Zodiac. Quiet "accumulated strength" is the nature of their soul. Those born into Snake years are inclined toward the abstract and aesthetic in life. Unusually gifted with deep intuitions, Snakes are the consummate philosophers. Insight, compassion, subtlety, and discretion are the sum and substance of this sixth sign of the Eastern Zodiac. The highly sensual Snake is possessive and needs an emotional partner who abandons themselves to feelings and passionate desire. The most harmonious time of day for the Snake is between the hours 9 a.m. and 11 a.m.

Famous Snakes:

Condoleeza Rice
Sarah Michelle Geller
Dean Martin
Charlie Sheen
Oprah Winfrey
Howard Hughes,
Martin Luther King, Jr.
Princess Grace Kelly Rainier

The Talkative Horse (Wu)

January 25, 1906 to February 12, 1907: Fire Horse
February 11, 1918 to January 31, 1919: Earth Horse
January 30, 1930 to February 16, 1931: Metal Horse
February 15, 1942 to February 4, 1943: Water Horse
February 3, 1954 to January 23, 1955: Wood Horse
January 21, 1966 to February 8, 1967: Fire Horse
February 7, 1978 to January 27, 1979: Earth Horse
January 27, 1990 to February 14, 1991: Metal Horse
February 12, 2002 to January 31, 2003: Water Horse
January 31, 2014 to February 18, 2015: Wood Horse

The Horses are the physically active, oratory, and quick-witted athletes of the Zodiac. Charming, independent, and decisive, the Horse prefers to be "on the move," with places to go and people to see. Natural leaders, Horses are idealistic and humanitarian in character, as well as gifted speakers and strong communicators. Elegant, witty, and charming, those born into Horse years are difficult to defeat in an argument and always make a persuasive case. Often successful in politics or public speaking, the cheerful and friendly Horse is effusive, and needs absolute freedom to maneuver through life's pastures. This independent seventh sign of the Zodiac requires a mate who stimulates their mind and appreciates their wit. The rejuvenating time of day for Horses is between 11 a.m. and 1 p.m.

Famous Horses:

Sean Connery

John Travolta

Clint Eastwood

Ulysses S. Grant

Theodore Roosevelt

Frederic Chopin

Aretha Franklin

Kevin Costner

The Artistic Goat (Wei)

February 13, 1907 to February 1, 1908: Fire Goat

February 1, 1919 to February 19, 1920: Earth Goat

February 17, 1931 to February 5, 1932: Metal Goat

February 5, 1943 to January 24, 1944: Water Goat

January 24, 1955 to February 11, 1956: Wood Goat

February 9, 1967 to January 29, 1968: Fire Goat

January 28, 1979 to February 15, 1980: Earth Goat

February 15, 1991 to February 3, 1992: Metal Goat

February 1, 2003 to January 21, 2004: Water Goat

February 19, 2015 to February 7, 2016: Wood Goat

Goats are artists in temperament and in character. These changeable free spirits love social gatherings, stimulating conversation, and interesting people. "Propriety" and a beautiful environment are important to their souls. Gentle in spirit, Goats desire a peaceful spot where they can exist undisturbed and without obligation. Creative, sensitive, and kind, those born into Goat years are warmhearted, disorganized, and extremely vulnerable. They are capricious, work when least expected to, and are never reached by being pressured. The eighth sign of the Zodiac, the Goat is intelligent, sometimes insecure, and always generous to a fault. Good Samaritans, they have a soft heart towards those less fortunate, whether a homeless puppy or a needy friend, and need a strong partner who is able to take the reins and handle their usually fortunate finances. Goats gather strength between the early afternoon hours of 1 p.m. and 3 p.m.

Famous Goats:

William Shatner
Bruce Willis
Julia Roberts
Chow Yun Fat
Bill Gates
Pamela Anderson
Mick Jagger
Michelangelo
Leonardo da Vinci

The Entertaining Monkey (Shen)

February 2, 1908 to January 21, 1909: Earth Monkey
February 20, 1920 to February 7, 1921: Metal Monkey
February 6, 1932 to January 25, 1933: Water Monkey
January 25, 1944 to February 12, 1945: Wood Monkey
February 12, 1956 to January 30, 1957: Fire Monkey
January 30, 1968 to February 16, 1969: Earth Monkey
February 16, 1980 to February 4, 1981: Metal Monkey
February 4, 1992 to January 22, 1993: Water Monkey
January 22, 2004 to February 8, 2005: Wood Monkey
February 8, 2016 to January 27, 2017: Fire Monkey

The youthful and clever Monkey is the eternal child of the Eastern Zodiac. These highly diverse and bright souls are irrepressible. Monkeys are quick, restless, enterprising, and sexual. Mischievous and high-spirited, Monkeys are social, active, convincing, and are gifted with a hilarious sense of humor. Imagination, ingenuity, and resourcefulness characterize those born into a year of the multifaceted Monkey. Versatile, curious, and easily bored, impish Monkeys are witty companions. They are indulgent, intelligent, and always ready to play. This ninth sign of the Zodiac is the most difficult to define due to their dual and sometimes contradictory nature. Monkeys need mentally sharp partners who stimulate their cerebral resources. The best time of day for Monkeys is between 3 a.m. and 5 p.m.

Famous Monkeys:

Jennifer Aniston
Lisa-Marie Presley
Tom Hanks
Harry Houdini
J.M. Barrie

David Copperfield
Michael Douglas
Milton Berle

The Industrious Rooster (You)

> January 22, 1909 to February 9, 1910: Earth Rooster
> February 8, 1921 to January 27, 1922: Metal Rooster
> January 26, 1933 to February 13, 1934: Water Rooster
> February 13, 1945 to February 1, 1946: Wood Rooster
> January 31, 1957 to February 17, 1958: Fire Rooster
> February 17, 1969 to February 5, 1970: Earth Rooster
> February 5, 1981 to January 24, 1982: Metal Rooster
> January 23, 1993 to February 9, 1994: Water Rooster
> February 9, 2005 to January 28, 2006: Wood Rooster
> January 28, 2017 to February 15, 2018: Fire Rooster

The Rooster is the military strategist and appearance-conscious soul of the Eastern Zodiac. Finely dressed and possessing a taste for pageantry, the Rooster enjoys a lively, outgoing manner, and is most candid in speech. These efficient and methodical souls work hard today, applying themselves and planning ahead for the rewards of tomorrow. Confident, resilient, and industrious, those souls born into Rooster years apply themselves to practical projects. Enthusiastic about details others may have overlooked, Roosters refuse to be bossed and are best suited for work over which they have control. Swanky Roosters may tend to boast a bit, but this 10th sign of the Zodiac is a reliable and excellent friend. Roosters love to socialize and adore adornment and finery. The assertive Rooster needs a strong and self-assured partner whom they can respect. The rejuvenating time of day for Roosters is between the sunset hours they rule, from 5 p.m. to 7 p.m.

Famous Roosters:

> Catherine Zeta-Jones
> Usama bin Laden
> John F. Kennedy
> Priscilla Presley
> Gloria Estefan
> Steve Martin
> Yoko Ono
> Groucho Marx

The Observant Dog (Xu)

> February 10, 1910 to January 29, 1911: Metal Dog
> January 28, 1922 to February 15, 1923: Water Dog
> February 14, 1934 to February 3, 1935: Wood Dog
> February 2, 1946 to January 21, 1947: Fire Dog
> February 18, 1958 to February 7, 1959: Earth Dog
> February 6, 1970 to January 26, 1971: Metal Dog
> January 25, 1982 to February 12, 1983: Water Dog
> February 10, 1994 to January 30, 1995: Wood Dog
> January 29, 2006 to February 3, 2007: Fire Dog
> February 16, 2018 to February 4, 2019: Earth Dog

Dogs are the watchful worriers of the Chinese Zodiac and the champions of the underdog. The Dog is known for its complete loyalty toward their friends and loved ones, and their viciousness toward the enemies of their loved ones. Anxiety, loyalty, and protectiveness characterize the magnanimous Dog personality. Devotion, generosity, and perseverance are the cornerstones of the wary Dog's temperament. This 11th sign of the Eastern Zodiac is earnest, sincere, and faithful to those whom they love. However, as they are often plagued by wariness, they can have a sharp tongue and tend to jump to conclusions. Cautious and serious regarding love, the Dog needs a trustworthy partner with strong family sympathies and an appreciation of their tenderhearted virtues. Low on ego, high on soapboxes, the Dog's fair-minded humanitarianism and extreme caution is legendary. The best time of day for Dogs is between 7 p.m. and 9 p.m.

Famous Dogs:

Madonna
Michelle Pfeiffer
Elvis Presley
Winston Churchill
Gary Oldman
George W. Bush
Cher
Brittany Spears

The Honest Pig (Hai)

> January 30, 1911 to February 17, 1912: Metal Pig
> February 16, 1923 to February 4, 1924: Water Pig
> February 4, 1935 to January 23, 1936: Wood Pig
> January 22, 1947 to February 9, 1948: Fire Pig
> February 8, 1959 to January 27, 1960: Earth Pig
> January 27, 1971 to January 15, 1972: Metal Pig
> February 13, 1983 to February 1, 1984: Water Pig
> January 31, 1995 to February 18, 1996: Wood Pig
> February 18, 2007 to February 6, 2008: Fire Pig
> February 5, 2019 to January 24, 2020: Earth Pig

Considerate, long-suffering, and supremely honest, the unpretentious Pig makes a cheerful friend and sincere partner. This 12th and last sign of the Zodiac is pragmatic and has an unquenchable thirst for new knowledge. They are often betrayed because of their faith in others, but are many times rewarded with financial security due to their pure hearts. Companionship, physical love, and emotional security are a must, and these souls need an easy-going mate who talks out problems instead of shouting. Gentle yet strong of will, Pigs are motivated by their conscience. Resigned and accepting of the world as it is, Pig souls do not push themselves ahead at the cost of another. The most harmonious time of day for the Pig is between 9 p.m. and 11 p.m.

Famous Pigs:

The Dalai Lama
Stephen King
Noah Wyle
Arnold Schwarzenegger
Luciano Pavarotti
Ralph Waldo Emerson
Carl G. Jung
Tracey Ullman

Endnotes

Chapter 1

1. Feng shui is the Chinese art of placement. Literally translated as wind and water, feng shui utilizes the principals of the five elements to choose harmonious shapes, colors and directions to achieve balance and harmony.

2. Myers-Briggs or the MBTI(r) is the most widely used modern personality-type indicator. It is the most popular instrument for measuring a person's preferences, using four basic scales with opposite poles.

Index

B

balance, finding, 15
birth hour, 189-194
birth sign chart, 18-22
Book of Changes. *See* Yi Jing
Buddha, 17

C

character vs. temperament, 12
Chen. *See* Dragon
Chou. *See* Ox
combatants vs. soul mates, 199-201
compatibility trines, 196-198
Confucius, 13

D

destiny, 14
Doctrine of the Five Elments, the, 164-165
Dog,
    career choices for, 146
    child, 145
    duality of, 143
    famous examples of, 146-147
    gifts of, 144
    home life of, 145
    love and, 228-231
    man, 150-152
    temperament of, 142-143
    woman, 147-150

Dragon,
    career choices for, 75
    child, 74
    duality of, 72
    famous examples of, 75
    gifts of, 72-73
    home life of, 74
    love and, 213-215
    man, 78-79
    temperament of, 71-72
    woman, 76-78

E

Earth, element of, 176-177
Earth-element combinations, 177-179
Earthly Branch vs. Heavenly Branch, 163-187
Eastern astrology vs. Western astrology, 11-12
Elements Chart, 187
elements, the, 163-187
    creative cycles, 165
    destructive cycles, 165

F

fate, 14
feng shui, 14

251

Fire, element of, 172-173
Fire-element combinations, 173-176

G

Goat,
  career choices for, 110
  child, 109
  duality of, 107-108
  famous examples of, 110-111
  gifts of, 108-109
  home life of, 109-110
  love and, 221-223
  man, 114-116
  temperament of, 106-107
  woman, 112-114

H

Hai. *See* Pig
Heavenly Branch vs. Earthly Branch,
  163-187
Horse,
  career choices for, 98
  child, 97
  duality of, 96
  famous examples of, 99
  gifts of, 96-97
  home life of, 98
  love and, 218-220
  man, 102-103
  temperament of, 94-96
  woman, 100-102
hou tian, 12

I

I Ching, 14
incompatibility, 198-199

K

Kongzi, 13

L

Laozi, 13, 15
love signs, 194-234
luck, 14

M

Mao. *See* Rabbit
meaningful coincidences,
  theory of, 11
Metal, element of, 179-180
Metal-element combinations,
  180-183
ming yun. *See* fate
ming. *See* destiny
Monkey,
  career choices for, 121-122
  child, 120-123
  duality of, 119-120
  famous examples of, 122
  gifts of, 120
  home life of, 121
  love and, 223-226
  man, 125-127
  temperament of, 118-119
  woman, 123-121
Myers-Briggs, 16

O

Ox,
  career choices for, 40
  child, 38-39
  duality of, 37
  famous examples of, 40
  gifts of, 38
  home life of, 39-40
  love and, 205-208
  man, 43-45
  temperament of, 37
  woman, 41-43

P

personality traits, 12

Pig,
   career choices for, 157-158
   child, 156-157
   duality of, 155
   famous examples of, 158
   gifts of, 155-156
   home life of, 157
   love and, 231-234
   man, 161-162
   temperament of, 154-155
   woman, 159-160

Q

Qi. *See* spirit.

R

Rabbit,
   career choices for, 62
   child, 61
   duality of, 59-60
   famous examples of, 62
   gifts of, 60-61
   home life of, 61-62
   love and, 210-213
   man, 65-68
   temperament of, 58-59
   woman, 63-65

Rat,
   career choices for, 28
   child, 27
   duality of, 26
   famous examples of, 29
   gifts of, 26-27
   home life of, 28
   love and, 202-205
   man, 32-34
   temperament of, 24-26
   woman, 30-31

Rooster,
   career choices for, 133
   child, 132-131
   duality of, 131
   famous examples of, 134
   gifts of, 131
   home life of, 133
   love and, 226-228
   man, 137-139
   temperament of, 130-132
   woman, 135-136

S

Sha Chi, 50
Sha Qi, 16
Shen. *See* Monkey
Sheng Qi, 16
Si. *See* Snake
Snake,
   career choices for, 85-86
   child, 84-85
   duality of, 83
   famous examples of, 86
   gifts of, 83-84
   home life of, 85
   love and, 215-218
   man, 89-91
   temperament of, 82-83
   woman, 87-89
soul mates vs. combatants, 199-201
spirit, 15, 16
synchronicity, spiritual laws of, 11
Tai Ji, 15
Tao Ti Jing, 15
Tao, 15, 16
temperament vs. character, 12
Tiger,
   career choices for, 51
   child, 50
   duality of, 49
   famous examples of, 52

gifts of, 49-50
home life of, 51
love and, 208-210
man, 54-56
temperament of, 48-49
woman, 53-54
Triangles of Compatibility, 196
Tse, Lao, 11, 13, 17
Tze. *See* Rat

W

Water, element of, 183-184
Water-element combinations, 184-186
Wei. *See* Goat
Western astrology vs. Eastern astrology, 11-12

Wood, element of, 169
Wood-element combinations, 170-172
Wu. *See* Horse

X

xian tian, 12
Xu. *See* Dog

Y

yang forces, 167-169
yang vs. yin, 15, 16, 163
Yi Jing, 14
yin forces, 166-167
yin vs. yang, 15, 16, 163
Yin. *See* Tiger
You. *See* Rooster

About the Author

Like most of those born into a year of the defending Dog, Shelly Wu spent a fair amount of her childhood fighting bullies and taking up the gauntlet for the picked on and the friendless. Wu no longer scuffles with bullies, but she still climbs upon her soapbox. She adheres to the words of Lao Tse: "In the perception of the smallest is the secret of clear vision; in the guarding of the weakest is the secret of all strength."

Wu's horoscope columns and feature articles have appeared in *A. Magazine: Inside Asian America, The Rainbow News, The Tea Leaf, Psychic Interactive, Your Stars, In Touch, and Life* magazines. Wu's articles have also been featured in the Associated Press, on ABC

News, and the BBC. Her yearly Chinese astrology predictions are carried on the Wireless Flash news service.

Wu has studied and taught Chinese astrology and the arcane sciences for many years. Her mentor was her father, a spiritual leader and teacher.

Wu brings her knowledge to the Online College of Astrology, where she teaches Chinese astrology in the Certification Preparation Department. Since 1995, she has presented this ancient art via the World Wide Web and maintains a popular Website at *www.chineseastrology.com*.

Wu has been dubbed the "Dear Abby" of Chinese astrology and can be heard on radio talk shows world wide.